Traps &

More Trap Making

Step by Step

Plans, tips and ideas

By

John Bryan

This book is dedicated to all the men, women and young people who are
keeping traditional country skills alive through their
enthusiasm, friendliness and willingness to share.

I would like to thank all those who have contributed to this book with
corrections, suggestions and the use of their photographs.

I would particularly like to thank Callum and Bryden of
Aith Junior High School, Shetland
for their help testing the Mouse Funnel Trap plans.

Get the work level and resting on something solid.

ISBN: 978-0-9558535-1-7

SECTION 2   TRAP MAKING PROJECTS

SECTION 3   REVISITING 'TRAP MAKING, STEP BY STEP'

More Trap Making – Step by Step

Introduction

As this book goes to press it is just over four years since my first book, Trap Making Step by Step, was published. In all honesty I never expected to be able to write a second book on trap making, but it's surprising how quickly new material can build up once you allow yourself to see and develop it. What has helped is that I have been lucky enough to meet, talk to and correspond with many readers of that book, whose stories of their own trap making and the ideas which they have come up with are fascinating. From these conversations I have also gained a few suggestions, (such as the inclusion of more photographs), which I hope will make this book even more useful than the first.

In this book I have broadened the scope to include more than just trap plans. I have dealt with the most popular of the professional spring trap types, so that readers may use them with greater effectiveness. Use of the term 'humane trap' to mean a live catch trap has become very common in recent years, but in truth can often mean quite the opposite. A well prepared, well set spring trap of suitable power can kill an animal almost instantly. Compare that with a 'humane' cage trap in the hands of an amateur, who may not check the trap as frequently as he should and may not possess the skills or the resolve to dispatch the quarry in a quick and effective manner. With this in mind I have also discussed suitable methods for dispatching caught animals.

As with Trap Making Step by Step, it is always worth reading each chapter through to the end before you start any preparation. It will help enormously when you're following the plans if you understand how the final trap fits together. Also many of the options and variations require building in from an early stage and it can be frustrating to discover this after you've cut the wood.

More than anything I would encourage you to take this book as a starting point. Allow yourself to consider new ideas, experiment with materials and designs and don't be afraid to try things out. Stick within the law, keep the welfare of target and non-target animals as paramount and you won't go far wrong.

Legal and Moral Responsibilities

Anyone considering making and using any traps covered in this book must be aware of the legislation that applies to the target species (which may differ between regions) and be prepared to deal with any successful catches. UK law on trapping is complex and covered by a range of different Acts some of which are discussed below.

Traps should be inspected regularly and I recommend at least daily, ideally twice a day for a live catch trap. The UK Protection of Animals Act 1911 requires spring traps set for rabbits and hares to be checked daily but no other legislation sets a frequency requirement for Spring Traps. You could argue that if a kill trap is set correctly there should be no need to check daily, however, a miscatch would render the caught animal 'under the control of man' thereby triggering the Animal Welfare Act 2006. So my advice is to check your traps every day.

Any live catches should be either released or humanely killed and disposed of appropriately. It is unacceptable to prolong the suffering of any animal regardless of how much it may be regarded as a 'pest'. A cheap air rifle or an air pistol is an excellent tool for close range dispatch of captured target animals but must be used responsibly. The legislation covering the ownership and use of air guns is quite specific and advice covering the UK can be found on the BASC website. In some countries, such as the Republic of Ireland, a license is required.

Trappers must be familiar with the animals being targeted and be able to distinguish them from any which may be caught accidentally. The **Wildlife & Countryside Act 1981** (as amended) protects all wild birds and some wild animals and regulates the methods by which they can be controlled. But legislation such as the Wild Mammals (Protection) Act 1996 and the Animal Welfare Act 2006 ensure that certain welfare standards apply to all animals.

It's worth pointing out that grey squirrel are a non-native species, (like mink and signal crayfish), and under Sec 14(1)(b) of Wildlife and Countryside Act 1981 it is an offence to release or allow to escape into the wild, any animal which is included in Part I Schedule 9 of the Act. As such, grey squirrels must either be humanely dispatched or kept under licence. Conversely red squirrels are protected; they must be released unharmed if caught and if accidentally caught regularly trapping should be stopped in that area.

Another important piece of legislation in the UK is the **2006 Animal Welfare Act**. This was primarily aimed at pet owner and animal keepers makes them responsible for ensuring that the welfare needs of their animals are met. Any wild animal that you catch is automatically covered by this act and you are responsible for it. Under the act, it is an offence to cause unnecessary suffering to a kept animal so you must promptly release it or humanely dispatch it.

Specific to the use of spring traps is the **Spring Traps Approval Order**, which is covered in more detail in later chapters.

The control of magpies, crows, woodpigeons and other birds is restricted by law and is only permitted under specific General Licences issued annually by Natural England (www.naturalengland.org.uk/conservation), the Scottish Executive for Scotland (www.scottishexecutive.gov.uk), Welsh Assemble Government (www.wales.gov.uk) and Northern Ireland Environment Agency (www.doeni.gov.uk). General Licences reduce bureaucracy by allowing people to control protected species without the need to apply for a personal licence. If you plan to act under the authority of a General Licence, you must:

- **be satisfied that you are eligible to do so**. (eligibility is licence-specific and in most cases there is a condition preventing use of the licences by persons who are convicted of wildlife crimes after 01 January 2010)
- **act within the provisions of the relevant General Licence and therefore the law.** This means that it is your responsibility to read the conditions of the licence to ensure that your situation is covered, and to comply with these conditions. However, you do not need to carry a paper copy of the relevant General Licence.

The Licenses are usually renewed annually and it's your responsibility to keep up to date with changes.

The most commonly used licences are:

- Licence to kill or take certain birds to conserve wild birds.

- Licence to kill or take certain birds to preserve public health or public safety

- Licence to kill or take certain birds to prevent serious damage or disease (damage to livestock, foodstuffs for livestock, crops, vegetables, fruit, growing timber, fisheries or inland waters)

Take the time to find out the law for where you live.

General Terms, Materials and Techniques

Materials

The traps in this book are made using three main materials; plywood, roofing lath and wire mesh.

- Roofing Lath is the long timber strips used across roof beams to support the tiles. Typically 35mm wide by 18mm thick, this tanalised pine is sold in lengths of 2.4m or 4.8m from any timber yard or builders merchant. Being pressure treated it is already weather resistant and ideal for outdoor use.

- Where plywood is used it must be external grade, or even better marine grade. Although manufactured for outdoor use, plywood is a composite material and so has lots of gaps where moisture can get in and start to damage it. Plywood will always benefit from a couple of coats of preservative such as Cuprinol. Avoid strong smelling creosote at all costs as this will keep animals away for months.

- Wire mesh should be galvanised and about 19 gauge if being used to cover a wooden frame and 14 gauge for making self-supporting cages. Care should also be taken to select the correct mesh hole size and if in any doubt go smaller rather than larger. Rats and squirrels can comfortably fit though a 2 inch hole and will often pass through smaller ones. Mesh of the wrong size can also increase the chances of trapped animals injuring themselves.

Right   **Wrong**

When cutting mesh always measure and cut to whole squares, even if that means making the trap a little larger.

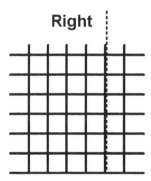 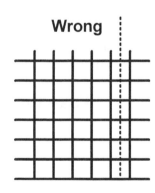

- Wood Glue
  Not really a material in its own right, a good quality, exterior grade wood glue is an essential element for all of the wood based projects.

Terms & Techniques

Joining Mesh	**Cage Making Clips** The simplest way to join mesh in a reliable, long lasting and professional looking way is to use cage making clips. The Fourteenacre shop sells cage clips in two sizes to cover a range of mesh thicknesses. **Cable Ties** A very popular and low cost approach is to use cable ties – a cheap, easy method that requires no special tools. Cable ties are a weak point in any cage where the trapped animal might be able to chew through them. Plastic ties will also degrade if exposed to weather and strong sunlight. **Lock Wire** A recognised technique for securing bolts and nuts in aeronautics and other industries where it is essential that fastenings remain secure. It can also be used very effectively to attach door supports, dividers and other framework to a mesh cage. Lock Wire pliers should be used to 'spin' and tighten the wire for a secure hold. 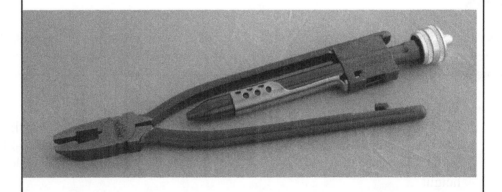 **Wire Twists** This is a cheap and temporary technique for securing mesh similar to the Lock Wire method. A short length of wire is threaded through two corresponding holes, wrapped around and then twisted together by hand. It is not recommended for anything other than emergency repairs or 'tacking' cages together in position while more reliable fixings are applied.
'Starting off' nails	This means hammering a nail part way through a piece of wood to get it 'started off' before getting all the pieces lined up. The advantage is that this gets the nails firmly in position so it's easier when you come to the final assembly.

Starter holes	Starter holes are a shallow holes made with a bradawl or similar that make it easier to start screws or screw fittings like screw eyes.
Pilot holes & Counter Sinks	Pilot holes are narrow diameter holes drilled in preparation for screws or nails to avoid splitting the wood. A counter sink is a small conical hole to allow the head of a screw or bolt to become level with the wood surface.

Tools

There are some basic tools which you really can't do without for these projects. Nothing too expensive and you probably have most of them at home already. There are also a few other project specific tools given at the start of some chapters.

- **Workbench.**
  Most important of all is somewhere to work. It doesn't have to be anything special and one of those fold-away workbenches available in DIY shops is ideal to start with. Any table or bench will do as long as it is level, stable and a comfortable working height.

- **Hammer.**
  Preferably a 'claw' hammer – the type with the two prongs on the back for removing nails.

- **Saw.**
  A good quality cross-cut wood saw - there's nothing worse for trying to cut neat, straight lines than a cheap, blunt saw.

- **Screwdriver.**
  Make sure that it's suitable for the screws you are going to use (i.e. slot or cross head).

- **Carpenters Square / Try Square.**
  This is something you might not have but well worth getting. It's a standard carpenter's tool used for marking lines at right angles to the edges of wood.

- **Marking Gauge.**
  Another carpenter's tool, this device is for marking lines parallel to the edge of a piece of wood. Again something you may not have but inexpensive and you'll wonder how you ever managed without one.

- **Coping Saw.**
  A saw with a thin blade held in between the arms of a 'U' shaped frame. This type of saw is used for cutting out shapes in solid pieces of wood. If you already have a jigsaw then that already does the job.

- **Wire Cutters.**
  Nothing too heavy-duty, just suitable for cutting the wire mesh.

- **Drill.**
  A hand or electric drill with a range of drill bits.

- **Bradawl.**
  A short pointed spike mounted in a handle – used to make starter holes for screws.

- **Staple Gun.**
  Not strictly essential but you'll find it much easier with one. A handheld staple gun will allow you to fix mesh quickly and neatly with one hand while positioning the mesh with the other.

- **Dremel**
  If you really want to do a first class job some people use a Dremel or similar rotary tool with a metal cutting disc to cut the weld mesh. This can take a bit longer and be a bit fiddly but it does give a really clean cut, tight against the edge of the mesh.

More Trap Making – Step by Step

SECTION 1

SPRING TRAPS & ACCESSORIES

Chapter 1 – Introducing
The 'Approved' Spring Trap

What is an 'Approved' Spring Trap ?

The term 'Spring Trap' is commonly used to describe any type of killing trap which is powered by a spring, for example the everyday mousetrap. The Pests Act 1954 makes it is an offence to use or permit the use of any spring trap, other than an approved trap, for the purpose of killing or taking animals. The Act also makes it an offence to use or knowingly permit the use of an approved trap in circumstances for which it is not approved e.g. as a pole trap. The Small Ground Vermin Traps Order 1958 goes on to exempt (i) spring traps known as break-back traps & commonly used for destruction of rats, mice or other small ground vermin and (ii) spring traps of a kind commonly used for catching moles in their runs.

The Spring Traps Approval Order was first introduced in 1957 as part of the legislation to outlaw traditional gin traps, (which caught animals by their limbs), and replace them with more humane, instant kill traps. The Order has been updated several times since then and anyone using spring traps should <u>be familiar with this Order and check regularly for updates</u>. Importantly at the present time the authorities in England, Wales, Scotland and Northern Ireland all publish their own version of the Approval Order. Although generally very similar, these are often published at different times and so can become out of step; e.g. a trap may be approved or withdrawn for use in Scotland but not yet in England. The published Orders are easily available on the internet.

It is important to understand that the Order is not only very specific about traps, but also about which species each trap can be used to catch and the manner in which the trap may be used. There is no such thing as a 'legal trap', only traps approved for use in specified circumstances.

These *Approved* spring traps, are a mainstay of gamekeepers, farmers and pest controllers in the control of ground predators like rats, stoats, weasels and grey squirrels. With the recent increase of smallholders, allotments and domestic chicken keeping at home, there are many people who could be buying these traps but without access to any handed down expertise. In this chapter I have set out to enable users of spring traps to get the best out of them and remain firmly within the law, as set out in the UK.

The traps with *Approved* status have gone through rigorous tests and government field trials and the manufacturers have a lot to lose if their products fall below standard. Unfortunately there are many cheap copies of these traps available, usually imported and of a low quality. The Order does allow for 'equivalent' traps to be used in place of the named manufacturers, but the terms are very strict and few, if any, of these copies would meet this condition:

"equivalent in all relevant respects to a spring trap of a type and make specified in the Schedule if it corresponds to the spring trap so specified in construction, in materials, in impact force or momentum, and in all other respects which are relevant to its effect or manner of operation as a trap"

While it is not currently an offence to sell substandard copy traps, it **is** an offence to use them, so it's safer to stick to the manufacturers named in the Order.

Over the next three chapters I have dealt in more detail with three of the most popular types of 'Approved' trap; the Fenn style, the bodygrip style and the Kania. Each chapter includes the basics of how to use the trap plus any accessories that are essential or just useful.

There are quite a few other traps included on the order and legal to use and these can generally be divided into two types;

- Older designs which are quite scarce and rarely used (e.g. Imbra and Juby Traps)

- Newer traps which are still establishing themselves in regular use (e.g. WCS Tube Trap, the DOC Traps and the Collarum)

General Preparation & Care

Out of the Box

Broadly speaking, there are two schools of thought on preparing your traps before first use. There are those who will tell you that your traps will work fine straight out of the box and into the field. By and large this is true and for small scale, quick and easy pest control many people will see doing anything more as unnecessary. For professional, large scale and long term use however, it is worth investing a little time up front to improve the effectiveness of your traps and prolong the life of your investment.

Tuning

Tuning traps is like tuning anything – it's about getting them to work as effectively and smoothly as possible. Any mass produced item is going to be a balance between the perfect product, the cost of production and the extent of what can be done mechanically. Traps as shipped from the factory do not necessarily have anything 'wrong' with them, but in some cases a small, manual tweak can improve them.

Degreasing

Brand new traps retain a residue of grease and dirt from the manufacturing process which can carry an unnatural scent, detectable by more sensitive animal noses. They will also be bright and shiny making them easier to spot, particularly by passersby. New traps can be 'degreased' by boiling in a mild detergent solution for about half an hour and then left outside to weather slightly. The traps can then be treated to either stain the surface and / or apply a protective coating. Boiling with natural materials such as oak bark or outer walnut husks will dye the traps very effectively. There are also many commercial trap dyes and coatings available from the USA including water soluble 'Black Crystal Dye' and 'Dakota Line Trap Dip' or 'Speed dip' which is applied by dipping traps in a mixture of Speed Dip and petrol. Traps can also be painted with dark colour aerosol car paint.

Storage and care

Always put your traps away clean, dry and unset. Don't leave them in the bottom of your game bag until the next time you want them – hang them up where the air can get round them until they're properly dry.

Store them away from strong smells. Traps left in the shed with the creosote or jeyes fluid will be useless until the smell fades again. Similarly watch for natural smells that can contaminate your traps – traps left near ferrets or ferreting equipment, of that have caught a mink, stoat or weasel will be no good for trapping rabbits or squirrels.

Periodically check the strength of the springs and separate out any trap that fails to make a clean kill when in use. Replace any traps that are too weak to deliver an instant kill.

Never test fire a trap with anything hard like a nail, stick or peg as this will bend the jaws and reduce the kill efficiency. Use a short length of the tubular foam insulation sold for lagging household water pipes.

Securing The Traps

Except for mole traps, most spring traps are supplied with securing chains, which should always be used. Securing your traps is important so that your catches (and traps!) are not carried away by an opportunistic predator. More importantly though, it is essential that no animal, accidentally foul caught or of a non-target species, is able to drag the trap away with them. An animal allowed to escape with a trap attached would be completely unacceptable.

Chains can be secured to fixed items in the area (trees, fence posts etc), to the tunnel or cubby (provided that is also secured) or to suitable wooden or metal pegs. It pays to have a variety of pegs, extension cables and fixings prepared so that you can use the best option in any situation.

Pegs & Stakes

Fixing methods can also be as simple as a good hardwood or steel peg, usually with a securing cable and swivel. Pegs should be at least 7 inches long and the metal one shown in the photograph is closer to 11 inches.

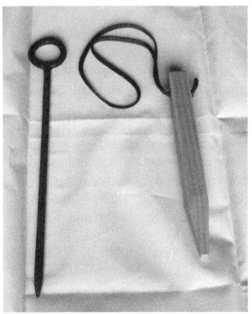

Some traps come with chains ready attached but a good supply of clips and securing cables is well worth having at hand. Cables should have loops or swivels at each end.

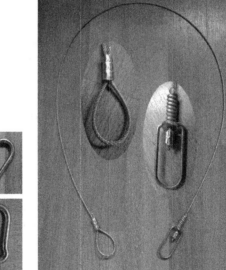

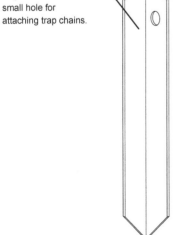

Angle Iron stake with small hole for attaching trap chains.

Simple heavy duty pegs or stakes can be made from ordinary angle iron, cut to a point and with a hole drilled in to attach the traps.

A stake made from steel reinforcing bar can be used with a swivel to allow full movement around the stake without the cable or chain getting tangled. A heavy washer or nut welded to the top prevents the swivel from slipping off the top.

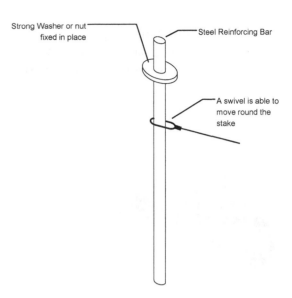

Reinforcing bar is mild steel and so rusts fairly easily. This roughening of the surface can lead to the swivel binding on and no longer moving round the stake. This should be checked regularly and the stake replaced or cleaned as necessary. The rebar stakes shown here have been painted to make them less visible and to prolong their working life.

Anchors

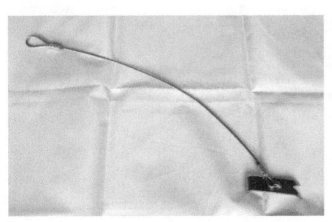

An idea common in the USA and becoming increasingly popular in the UK is what are referred to as Earth Anchors. These simple but ingenious devices are attached to a securing cable and are usually irretrievable. They're designed so that they can be pushed into the ground easily in one direction, but when the cable is pulled the anchors lock against the soil. The secret is in their shapes which are usually thin or pointed in one way and 'flat' the other.

There are several different designs of anchors available commercially and many are easy to replicate yourself if you have the time and equipment. There most common designs are shown here - Clockwise from top left: the Iowa, the Pogo, the Bullet and the Berkshire Stake

All anchors require a 'driver' to enable them to be hammered into the ground while maintaining the correct orientation. For the Berkshire Stake and Bullet this is a simple a metal rod with a blunt point, but for the Iowa something a little more sophisticated is required.

This version of an Iowa style anchor has been made from metal electrical conduit tube.

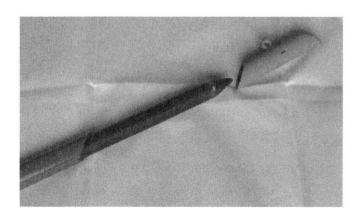
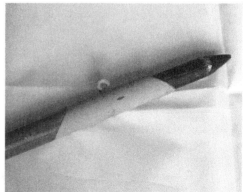

Chapter 2 - Fenn Style Traps

The name of A.A. Fenn & Co was established during the 1950s and was a very familiar brand from the 1960s right through to the end of the century, famous for quality spring traps, mole traps and cage traps of numerous types and designs. The most popular and enduring of the Fenn products are the Mark IV and Mark VI Spring Traps, designed for killing mammals in tunnels and on a level surface. The Mark IV is approved for use on grey squirrels, stoats, weasels, rats, mice while the slightly larger and more powerful Mark VI is approved for mink and rabbit in addition to those listed for the Mark IV.

There are now three manufactures of this style of trap who are named on the Approval Order; Fenn, Springer and Solway.

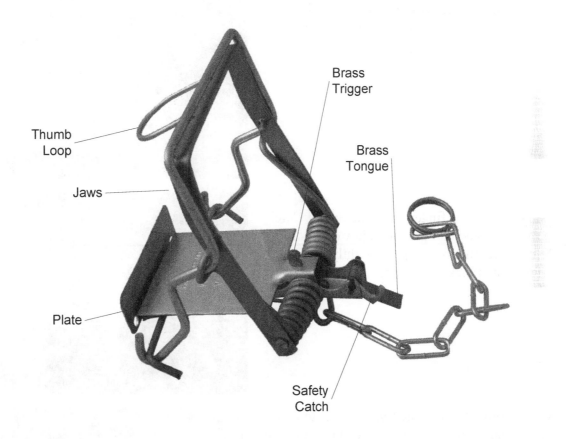

Basic Operation

How to set

The following photographs show the correct ways to set and release the Fenn Spring Trap. The methods are exactly the same for the Mark IV and the Mark VI but I recommend that first time users begin with the weaker Mark IV trap until they are familiar with the method. Most instructions for setting these traps show someone else setting the trap. In these photographs I've tried to show it as it looks when you are setting it. There is a short video on the Fourteenacre website showing this process.

Step 1

Place the trap in front of you with the springs on the right hand side. (If you're left handed you might want to swap the whole trap round, but the process is the same. Make sure that the brass Tongue and the Safety Catch hook are flicked back and that the chain is out of the way. Take the trap in your left hand with your fingers under the base of the trap and your thumb in the Thumb Loop.

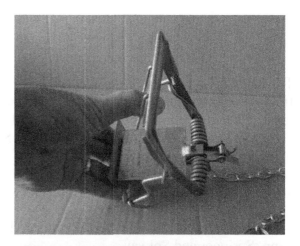

Step 2

With your left hand squeeze together and the jaws of the trap will begin to open. At this stage you can use your right hand to assist, mirroring the action of your left.

Step 3

Using your index finger, raise the Safety Catch so that it hooks onto the round jaw of the trap. Release pressure on the jaws slightly so that the Safety Catch locks into place.

At this point although the trap is under tension, it is in a safe condition and you can put it down or transport it. However you should not leave it like this long term as it will damage the springs. It is also still potentially dangerous, particularly to anyone unfamiliar with these traps, so should not be left unattended.

Step 4

To prepare to set the trap, rest the brass Tongue against the round jaw.

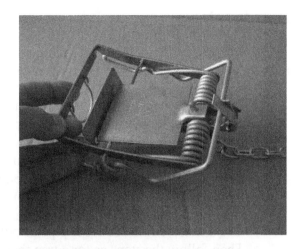

Hold the trap with your left hand and with your right thumb push down on the brass Tongue. You'll feel the jaws move and the Tongue will push down flat. Using your right index finger, push the plate upwards from underneath until the small brass notch on the plate slides over the end of the Tongue. The Trap is now set.

During this step the Safety Catch will become loose. By holding the trap at a slight angle you can ensure that it stays hooked over the jaw – then if you do have a problem the chances are that it will still hold the trap and save your fingers.

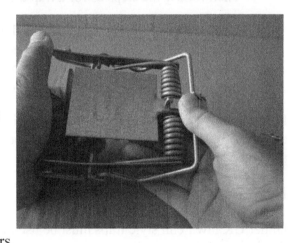

This final picture shows the trap fully set and with the Safety Catch still engaged. **When placed in a tunnel the trap should be this way round as an animal approaches it – that is the springs should always be to the side.**

Always leave the Safety Catch over the jaws until the trap is fully positioned and you are ready to leave. Then carefully flick it out of the way, ideally with a 'setting stick'.

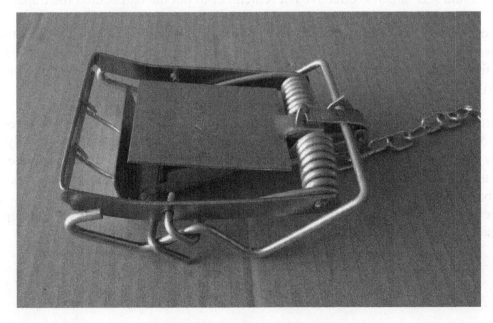

How to release

As mentioned earlier, spring traps should never be triggered using a stick or other hard object. If an untriggered trap needs to be released here are three suggestions that work well:

1) Remove the tunnel so that the trap can be accessed. Wearing stout shoes or boots place your foot squarely over the trap, making sure that your foot is covering the full length of the trap.
Push down firmly with your foot, (but don't put your weight on it), until you feel the trap fire. Slowly tip your foot back on your heel allowing the jaws to close in a controlled way against the sole of your shoe.

2) Use a short length of rubber pipe or polyurethane pipe insulation to trigger the trap. Then follow the steps as for a trap that has caught.

3) Engage the safety catch and trigger the trap. Holding the trap as you would to set it and reverse the setting process: Squeeze the trap enough so that you can tilt it and disengage the safely catch. Using your thumb and fingers slowly allow the jaws of the trap to close. Avoid letting it go suddenly as that likely to get you hurt.

Dealing with a trap that has caught is very similar to setting it in the first place. Hold the trap as you would to set it and open the jaws enough to allow the capture to fall out. Then slowly allow the jaws of the trap to close.

How and where to use

Under UK law Fenn style traps must be used in tunnels, and in fact in order to work properly the design of the trap relies on the presence of a tunnel roof at the correct height. That is, there should be hardly any gap above the jaws when closed. The Fenn traps were originally developed to be used on the ground and although there are now some innovative ideas for using Fenns 'off the ground' they still need to be set a flat, level surface.

Fenn traps work well in both 'run through' tunnels set along runs, against walls, between straw bales or on natural or artificial bridges. Tunnels that are blocked at one end and baited, known as 'blind sets' are also effective but remember to put the bait behind the trap.

The tunnel itself will be about 150mm to 180mm wide to accommodate the trap, but the entrances to your tunnels should be restricted to suit the animal you're targeting. This can be done by fixing ends with cut-outs onto your tunnel or by simply pushing sticks into the ground to partially block it, known as 'fencing'.

When setting on soft ground it is essential to clear the spot where you're going to place the trap, remove any loose debris that might prevent the plate from pushing down. Ideally create a shallow hole in which to 'bed' the trap as this makes it less visible and puts the plate level with the tunnel surface. When setting traps in natural tunnels, such as rabbit burrows, fine soil can be sieved over the trap to disguise it further, but be sure to remove any stones. Some trappers even place a square of tissue or paper over the plate, out to the jaws of the trap, to prevent soil falling through and going under the trap.

The trap should always be pegged down, using the chain provided and a wooden or metal peg. Wooden pegs should be made of a good hardwood like ash or hazel and about 7 inches long. The most common reason for securing the trap this way is to prevent any catches being carried off by larger predators, so make sure the peg is in firmly. A less common, but more important reason is to ensure that any mis-caught and injured animal cannot carry the trap away. With trap and animal still at the trap site you'll be able to manage the situation and the welfare of the animal, be it a non-target species or a foul caught target.

Tunnels & Boxes

Natural tunnels can be made in situ from the materials to hand at the site. This can be almost anything provided you can create the right sized tunnel; fallen or cut logs, bricks and rocks all make good tunnels. Although time consuming to make initially, this type of tunnel blends well into the habitat, is likely to hold familiar and interesting scents and of course, once built, can be reused season after season. A well built tunnel should blend into the site as much as possible but these photographs use a set built out in the open to show the simple steps required.

Clear an area to bed the trap and check that it fits properly: flat, stable and jaws level with the tunnel floor.

Place the logs, bricks or whatever you're using, either side of the trap and check that they form sides tall enough to allow the trap to fire without a large gap above the jaws. If you want to, now is the time to cover the trap with fine soil. You can also add 'jump rails' which encourage the target to land firmly on the trigger plate.

Begin covering over the tunnel and use sticks pushed into the ground to restrict the size of the opening. This 'fencing' minimises the risk of non target animals entering your set and is an important part of any set.

Complete the tunnel by adding the final parts of the tunnel roof.

More examples of tunnels built from natural materials:

A rock tunnel covered in straw.

A wooden tunnel covered and disguised with rocks, near to a game bird feeder.

Note the 2 inch mesh grill as very effective fencing to exclude non target species.

A classic set, alongside a stone wall. Many predatory mammals follow along walls and ditches and are attracted to rock piles where walls have started to collapse as these are often home to rodents.

Mesh tunnels have the advantage that they are prepared in advance and so traps can be placed in just a few minutes. Mesh is light weight and tends to stack better than wooden tunnels, but the dark enclosed nature of wooden tunnels seems to be more effective. Mesh tunnels should be covered with sacking, foliage or undergrowth to improve their effectiveness.

Wooden tunnels

Trap Making Step by Step includes plans for a basic wooden tunnel and an alternative design is shown here. Wooden tunnels can be made very simply from 2 sides and a top and then sited and fenced just like the natural tunnels described above. For ease of use or in environments where there may be children or pets more enclosed tunnels can be used with built-in jump rails either side of the trap, access restrictors on the tunnel ends and an access hatch.

Jump Rails

In a tunnel with a built in base, or when trapping on a hard surface, jump rails are an important technique in achieving a clean catch. Even when set, the Fenn trap has quite a high profile if viewed from the approaching animal's perspective, as this photo clearly shows.

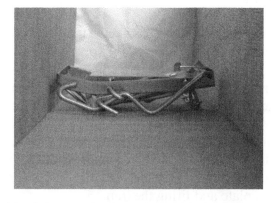

Ideally you want the target animal to bound onto the trap without hesitation to receive a firm and humane strike. So the less obvious the trap is the better. On soft ground you can create a hollow and bed the trap in, but where this is not possible jump rails are the answer.

By placing and firmly fixing strips of wood or small branches either side of the trap you create a platform level with the plate of the trap. In some cases the animal will simply jump up the step and land squarely on the trap plate. More cautious ones may investigate a little first, but will still be positioned correctly if they climb up slowly.

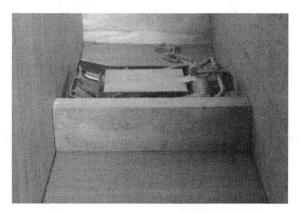

There are lots of different methods and materials that you can use, so be prepared to experiment. Two typical examples shown below are straight strips of wood and sections of feather edge board which create a gentle slope to the trap.

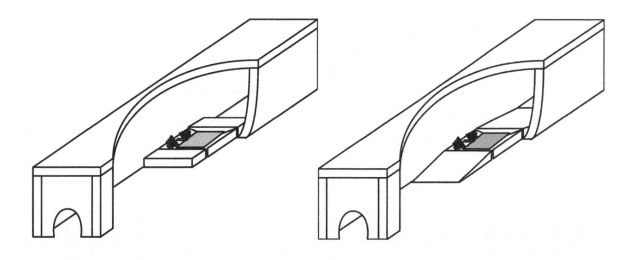

Boxes

More recently there has been a trend towards using Fenn style traps in self contained and movable boxes. There are two very good examples of these in *Modern Vermin Control*, one of the Gold Cockerel series of books by Michael Roberts. Michael demonstrates an 'Off The Ground' Fenn box for catching squirrels and an excellent ground level 'rat box' which is a very secure housing for a Fenn style trap.

James Linari-Linholm of JLL Pest Control, a full-time rural pest controller in Gloucestershire, has had a lot of success catching squirrels in top entrance boxes, built in sets of three. The bait is placed underneath the trap and squirrels enter through a hole in the top, landing on the trap plate and firing the trap.

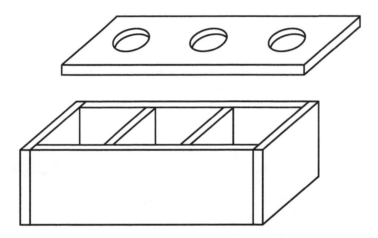

Another idea is a simple wooden box with lengths of drain pipe used as excluders. This is particularly suitable for rats.

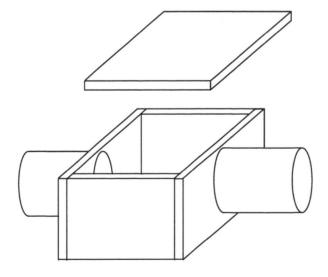

Accessories

Trapping Hammer

A traditional tool of trappers in the early 1900s the Trapping Hammer, Trap Setter or 'rabbiting hoe' still has a role with today's modern traps. Examples of an original and modern trapping hammer are shown here. An essential tool for knocking in the pegs to secure a trap, plus the notch in the blade serves as a 'chain pull' to remove the peg from the ground.

Characteristic of these hammers is the rear blade which is used for clearing a space to site a trap and to rake a flat area to bed the trap in.

Trapping Sieve

Trapping sieves are another traditional tool and a great help when disguising set traps - particularly in rabbit burrows. The simple sieve shown in the photographs can be made from four pieces of roofing lath or thin timber and a rectangle of 5mm square mesh.

It should be small enough to be held over a trap in a rabbit burrow and jiggled from side to side; to sift fine soil over the trap. Sieves can be made with higher sides to hold more soil, slightly tapered so that they fit more easily into the entrance of a burrow and even with a handle.

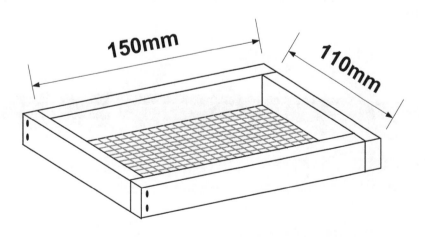

150mm

110mm

Setting stick

Another traditional trapper's tool, the setting stick is about 200mm to 250mm long, about 10mm thick and shaped to a wide, shallow point at one end.

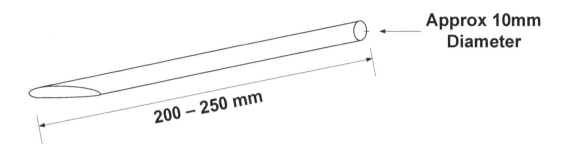

Approx 10mm Diameter

200 – 250 mm

When positioning and covering a Fenn trap, the shaped end of the stick is pushed under the plate to prevent the trap being accidently pushed down and the trap triggered.

At the final stage the stick is used to move the Safety Catch aside.

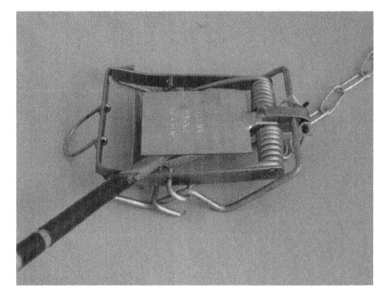

Like many traditional handmade items, setting sticks can be decorative as well as functional, as this example shows; supplied by Steve Caple, an experienced traditional trapper working in Northamptonshire.

Chapter 3 - Bodygrip traps

This style of trap is very popular and common in the USA with some very large and powerful sizes in use, (the Conibear 330 is strong enough to kill beavers and racoons). The BMI Magnum 55, 110 and 116 traps are specific variants that have been tested and approved for use under UK law and only these or their equivalents may be used. In fact the BMI Magnum 116 is specifically made just for the UK market.

The 55 is only legal to use on rats currently, while the 110 is approved for use on grey squirrels, stoats, weasels and rats. The more powerful 116 is approved for mink and rabbit, in addition to those listed for the 110.

The bodygrip family of traps are a little more complex to use than the Fenn style and cannot be just placed on the ground and covered by a simple tunnel. The two significant differences which need to be understood before using these traps are that:

a) The spring sticks out from the side of the trap and so the tunnel must allow for that while still restricting access by non target species when the trap is in place. It must also allow the trap to be manoeuvred into the tunnel when creating the set.

b) The traps are not able to stand up by themselves – a set trap must be supported either by the tunnel or by a separate alternative 'stand' or 'mount'. The more sophisticated tunnels used to enclose **and** support the bodygrip traps are often referred to as 'cubbies' or 'cubby tunnels'.

Although this may seem a bit daunting at first, with experience these complexities help to make the Bodygrip a highly versatile and adaptable trap.

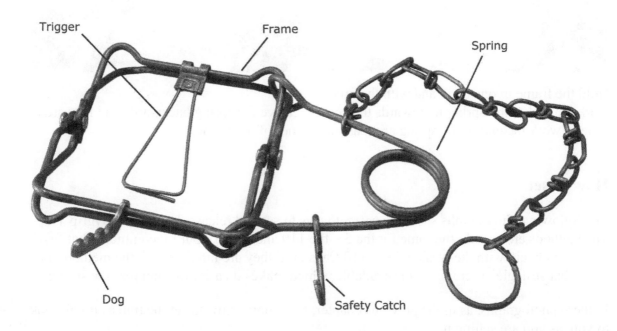

Basic Operation

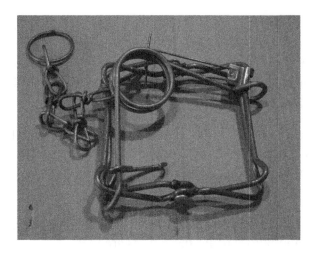

Spring Position

Occasionally you may get a trap where the spring is not quite in the right position, with one of the ends of the spring that has 'gone round the corner'. A trap like this is not broken and simply needs the spring brought back round to the side.

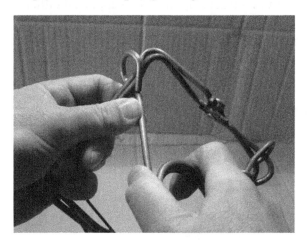 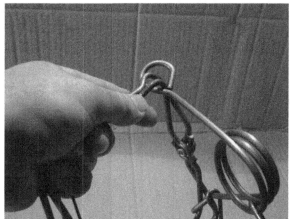

Hold the frame in one hand and with the other
work the end of the spring up towards the corner. Move the spring backwards and forwards a little to work the end of the spring arm past the corner of the frame.

How to set

The following photographs show the correct ways to set and release the BMI Bodygrip Trap. The methods are exactly the same for the 55, the 110 and the 116 but I recommend that first time users begin with the weaker 55 or 110 traps until they are familiar with the method. For those that struggle, a setting tool is available, which makes it easier to compress the spring.

In these photographs, as in the previous chapter, I've shown how to set the trap as it will look to you, as you are setting it.

There is also a short video on the Fourteenacre website showing how this done.

Step 1
Fold the spring out so that it's flat and straight out from the side of the trap.
Squeeze the spring together, bringing the two ends together.

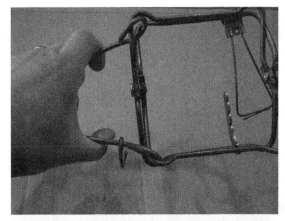

Step 2
If your hands are strong enough you may be able to squeeze the spring closed enough to clip the safety catch in place.

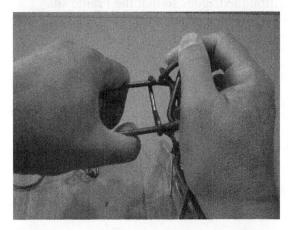

If you're not quite strong enough, you can use the frame of the trap to give you extra leverage. As the spring is compressed, pull trap frames together with other hand.

As above, engage the safety clip over both spring arms at the trap end of the spring.

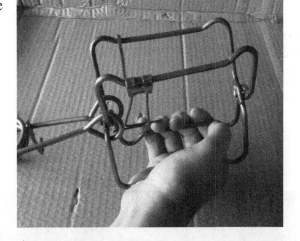

If you really find it difficult there are setting tools available.

Step 3
Having secured the spring, the frame of the trap will now be quite loose and will not close 'hard' on your fingers.

(In this photo the trap is shown in its side to give a clearer view.)

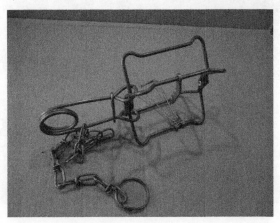

Step 4

Squeeze the two top edges of the frame together.

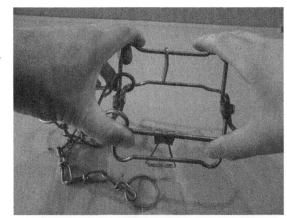

Step 5

Position the trigger so that the Frame sits properly in one of the notches of the Dog. Which notch you use will affect whether the trap is set 'heavy' (hard to trigger) or 'light' (more sensitive).

When the trap is in use, movement of the trigger wires will rotate the trigger around the frame, which will push the Dog upwards and dislodge the frame from the notch.

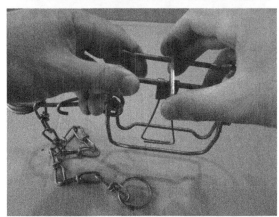

The trap is now set. Disengage the safety clip only when the trap is in position and ready to be left. The spring can be swung upwards if necessary to achieve a required setting position.

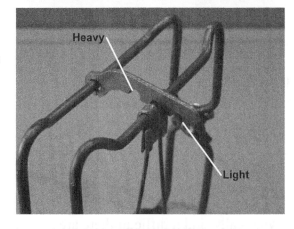

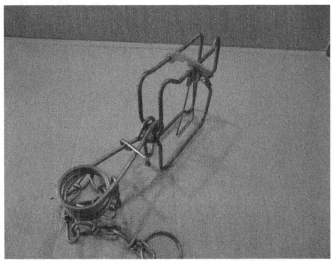

More Trap Making – Step by Step

How to release

As mentioned earlier, spring traps should never be triggered using a stick or other hard object.

To release the bodygrip trap you reverse the setting process:

- Re-engage the Safety Catch and keep your fingers well out of the way by handing the trap by the spring.

- Remove the trap from the stand and /or tunnel if possible.

- Once you can get to the trap safely, grip the bottom if the frame with one hand holding the two parts together. Hold the spring with your other hand.

- Shake the trap gently to disengage the dog from the trigger.

- Check that the Safety Catch is still in place. Keeping pressure on the spring and your fingers and thumbs out of the way, slowly allow the trap to close.

- To finish the release process, squeeze the spring and unhook the safety catch, before releasing the spring fully.

Fencing

Another useful feature of the bodygrip trap is that you can apply 'fencing' within the trap itself, to guide the target towards the trigger. A couple of well placed sticks between the kill bars on the inside will restrict the opening and ensure that the target pushes against the trigger. It is also very easy to slide the whole trigger mechanism over to one side and create an 'edge runner' set.

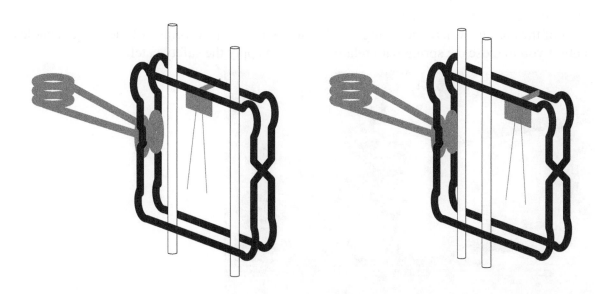

Accessories

Setting tool

The bodygrip family of traps includes some very powerful versions, (not legal for UK use), and these can be very difficult and dangerous to set by hand. This has led to the development of setting tools, which use a simple lever approach to make squeezing the spring easier.

Because bodygrip traps all work in the same basic way, these setting tools can also be used on the traps approved for use in the UK.

Using the Setting Tool

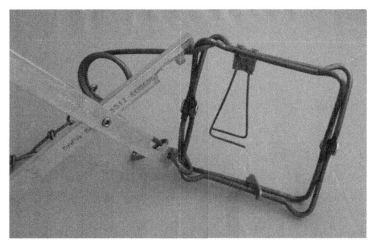

The notches at the end of the setting tool fit securely into the loops of the springs, where the spring attaches to the trap. The leverage of the longer handles enables you to close the spring with relative ease and apply the safety catch.

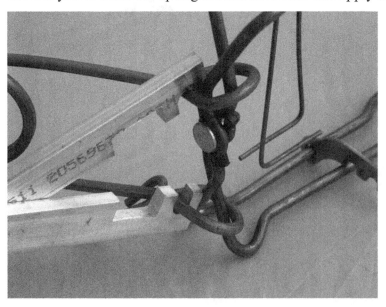

Extra-secure safety catches

The need for extra care on these larger traps has also lead to the development of more secure types of safety catch.

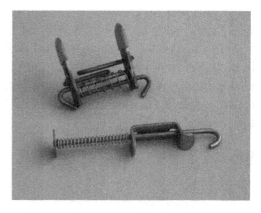

If you are nervous of using bodygrip traps then something like this can give you the confidence to become familiar with the traps.

Both the designs shown here use a pair of opposing hooks – spring loaded to keep them tight on the trap when it's set, but with 'stops' to catch the jaws if the trap fires. You also notice one of them has two pairs of hooks for different sized trap jaws.

Safety catches in place in a set trap.

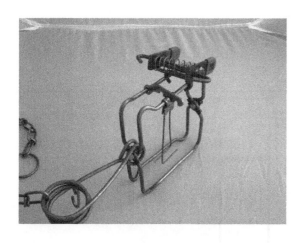
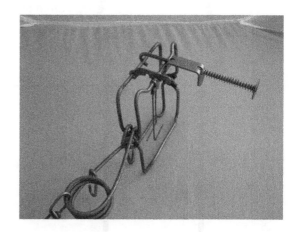

Safety catches having 'caught' a trap that has fired.

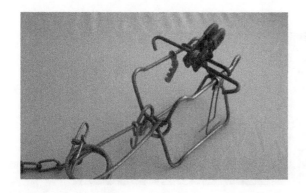
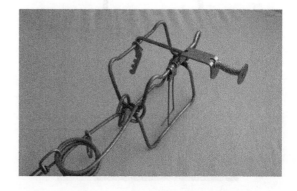

Stands, Mounts & Tunnels

There are a wide variety of stands and mounts that can be made cheaply and easily, and trapping books and websites from the USA show many inventive examples. Remember that in the USA trapping laws are different but in the UK none of these stands can be used without also using a covering tunnel. The advantage of using a stand though is that you can still mount a trap in a tunnel that you create from bricks, stones, logs and any other materials that are 'natural' to the trapping site.

Stands

Steel Rod Soft Ground Stand

This is a very strong stand usually made from three pieces of steel rod welded together. It has long legs that are pushed into the ground, with the cross bar resting at on the surface of the soil. The legs can be made a variety of lengths for use on different soil types.

The key measurements are those above the cross bar. The two 'elbows' of the stand need to be far enough apart to allow the hinges of the trap to fit inside. They also need to come back in far enough to support them from underneath but without blocking the route through.

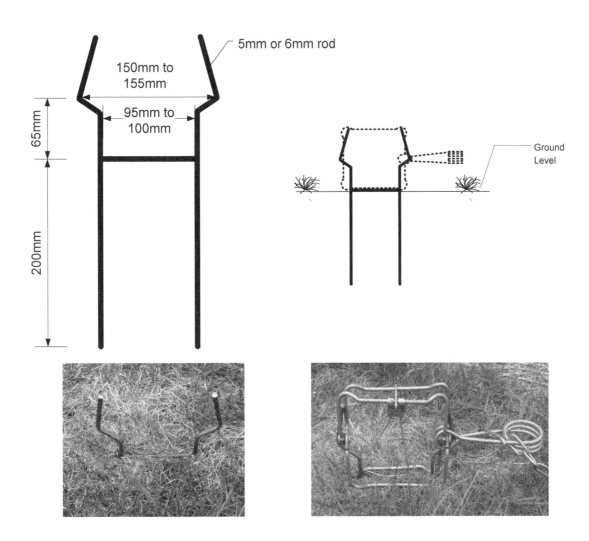

Wire Soft Ground Stand

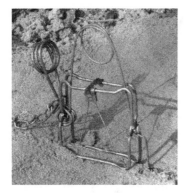

This stand is a similar shape and uses the same principle to support the trap. It is made from wire with shaped 'shoulders' to support the trap. In use it is pushed into the ground until the bottom of the trap is resting on the surface of the soil. The legs can be made a variety of lengths for use on different soil types.

What is crucial in this design is the height at which you place the loop as you do not want it to interfere with the trigger or the dog. In the shorter size the dog passes through the loop but has enough room within it to lift up when the trap fires.

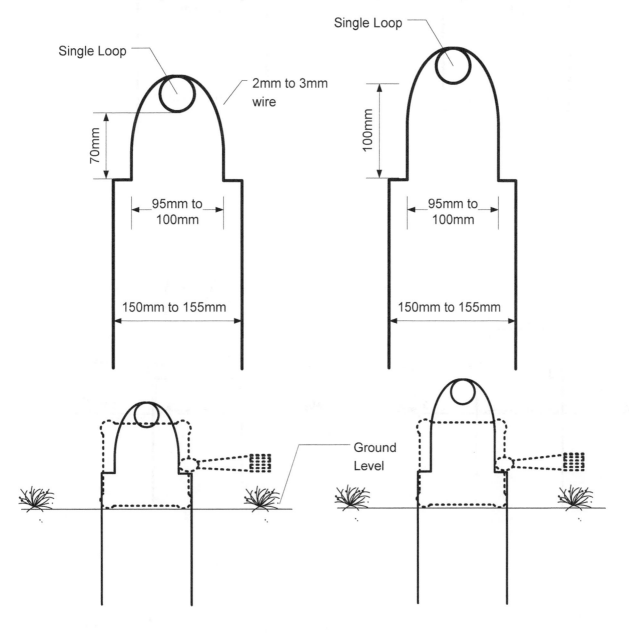

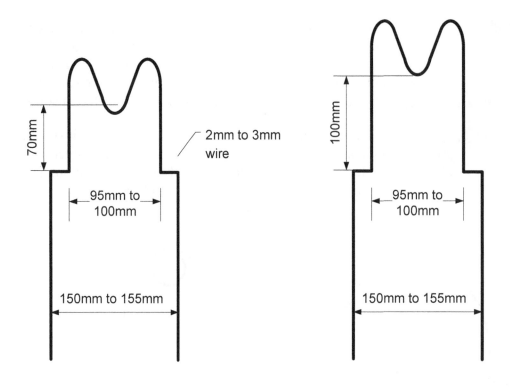

70mm

2mm to 3mm wire

95mm to 100mm

150mm to 155mm

100mm

95mm to 100mm

150mm to 155mm

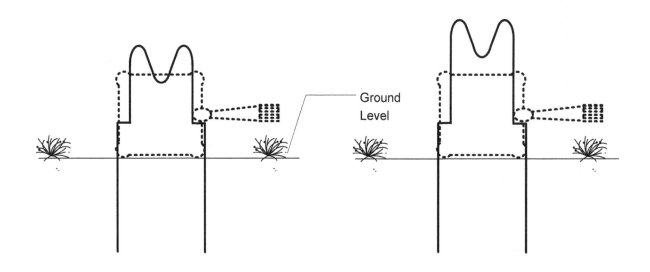

Ground Level

The best way to make these stands is to create a simple jig to form the wire round. This can be as easy as a board with stout nails hammered in at the correct places. Once you get a pattern that you're happy with it can be worth taking a bit of time to create a more permanent jig.

When you come to make the stand, thread the wire between the nails or pegs, bending it around the pegs as necessary to create the shape.

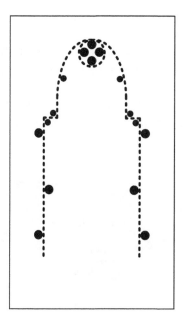

Mounts

One of the main advantages of the Bodygrip style of trap is that they are not restricted to being set flat on the floor. The 'gripping' frame can also be used to hold the trap in position if a suitable 'mount' is used where the frame comes together. When the trap fires, the frame moves outwards, releasing it from the mount.

As with Stands, there are many examples from the USA and Canada of mounting methods and once you've grasped the principle you'll probably think of some yourself. There are even commercial devices available but remember that for the UK you still need to be able to place and secure a tunnel.

Commercial Mounts & Stands

There are a variety of commercially produced mounts available from trapping stores in the USA. Many of these have online shops making it relatively easy to purchase these from the UK, although it can end up a bit expensive after postage is added. Some of the most popular types are shown here. You'll soon see that with a little ingenuity it's very easy to produce something just as good yourself. There are lots of commonly available metal channel, brackets and clips that can easily be adapted for use.

The 'killer clip'

A very popular, disposable clip made of uncoated spring steel. The clip comes with a pre-cut pair of integral spikes so that it can be hammered straight into the mounting surface.

Coni-mount bracket

One of the more professionally manufactured brackets, Coni-Mounts are made of steel and have holes located down the centre to permit fast, easy fastening.

These are available in varying designs and different sizes to accommodate the wider range of US traps. Shown here are the Coni-Bracket on the left and Barkers Coni-Mount on the right.

Screw in Stabiliser

Another simply made mount fitted to a threaded screw for ease of mounting.

Pocket Popper

No longer available, the Pocket Popper was designed to fit directly into the mouth of burrows and hole sets. A useful mount when trapping in natural tunnels

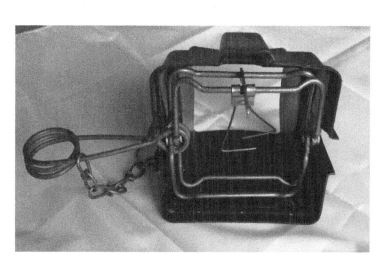

Self Made Mounts

When fitting a trap on a mount you will need to release it slightly so that it can be fitted into place. To do this make sure that the safety is in place on the spring, then grip the top of the trap frame and release the trigger. Keep a tight hold of the frame and allow it to open enough to fit into place. Then squeeze it back together and reset on the trigger.

In the following diagrams the spring, trigger and dog have sometimes been left off the drawings to improve clarity and because the mounts can be used with the spring on either side.

Nails in a plank

The simplest idea for a mount that I have ever seen is 4 wide headed nails hammered in a narrow rectangle. The same idea using a metal plate and bolts is useful in water sets as it won't float.

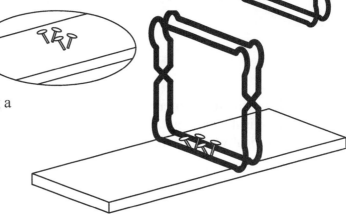

Wooden Slot Mount

A more robust but equally homemade alternative uses a 'T' section wooden block. This needs to be fixed firmly to a mounting surface so that between them, they create a slot for the two bottom sections of the trap frame.

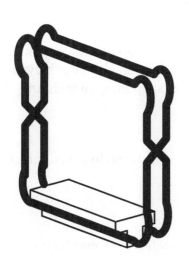

The mount should be made of hardwood and can either be routed or cut from a single block, or made by fixing two pieces together. The finished block should be about 80mm long and with the space underneath 15mm.

Something I've been thinking about, but not had chance to try yet, is making this block higher so that it can also become a bait holder. This would enable the trap to be baited and used as a double entry set.

Drilled Holes filled with bait

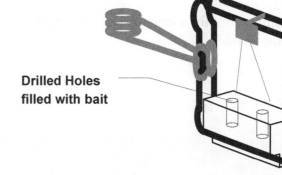

Tunnels

Tunnels for Body Grip traps are a little more sophisticated than those that you use for a Fenn style trap, but they're still quite straightforward once you understand what's required.

1. Allowing for the spring.
   Any bodygrip tunnel needs to make allowance for the side spring;

   - there must be enough room for the spring when the trap is set (either sticking straight out to the side or folded upwards).
   - there must be enough space for the spring to expand when the trap fires.
   - there must be a way of getting the trap and spring into the tunnel while the trap is set.

   What many newcomers to bodygrips don't realise is that once set, the spring can be swung up vertically next to the trap.

2. Allow for the Dog.
   There must be enough room for the Dog to move when the trap fires, else it may bounce back and foul the trap. If necessary cut a slot in the tunnel roof.

3. Support for the trap.
   As has already been discussed, bodygrip style traps need to be supported in the upright position when set. This can be done using a stand or mount but can also be achieved by building a support into the structure of the tunnel. These supporting tunnels are generally known as 'Cubby Tunnels'.

4. Restrict the catches.
   As with all trap tunnels, the entrances should be restricted so as to exclude non-target species.

The Basic Dimensions for a tunnel are about 2ft (600mm) long, 6 inches (155mm) high and 8 inches (200mm) wide.

Accommodating the Spring

These are 3 of the most common approaches to allowing for the spring in a bodygrip tunnel. They are shown here as mesh versions but they are just as suitable made from wood.

Classic 'T' cut out

Probably the most common method is to make a 'T' shaped slot in the side of the tunnel, at the point where the trap is going to be.

The stem of the 'T' needs to be wide enough to take the set spring, go all the way down and be open at the bottom.

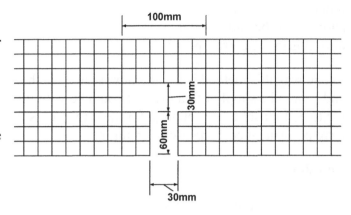

In use, the tunnel is simply placed over a trap that's already in a stand or mount, and the stem of the 'T' slid down over the trap spring.

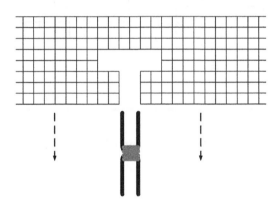

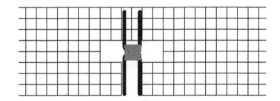

When the trap is fired, the spring spreads out sideways into the space provided by the head of the 'T'. If this is not wide enough it will prevent the spring opening fully and closing the trap.

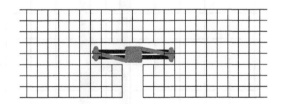

Long slot

This very similar method does away
with the vertical spring channel and
instead extends a slightly narrowed
slot all the way to the one end of the
tunnel. To set in place, the trap
spring must be slid along that slot
until it is in the correct position.

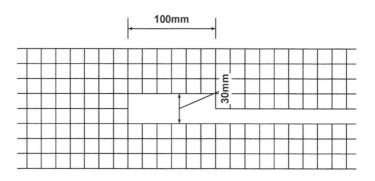

In one way this method is a little more secure, as the tunnel is much more difficult to remove
and cannot be simply lifted off as it could be with the 'T' design. However it also means that
the tunnel must be wide enough for the trap to pass through at one end, making it awkward to
have permanent entry restrictors built in.

Top slot

This design requires the smallest
cut out area from the tunnel and
crucially it's cut from the top not
the side.

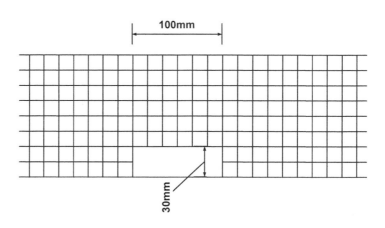

While the trap is set, the spring is folded upwards and sticks out from the top of the cage.

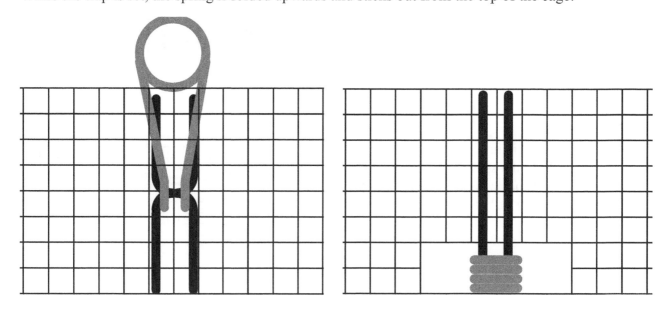

Side View   View from Above

When the trap fires, the spring is able to expand and fall into the tunnel.

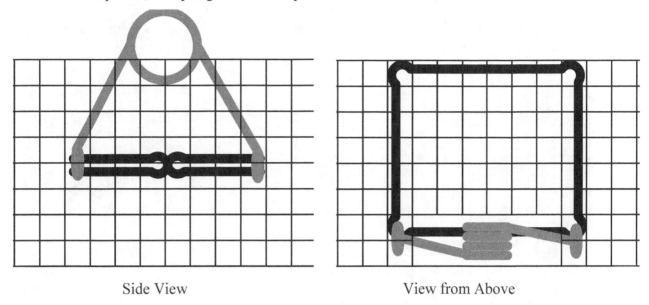

Side View   View from Above

Notice the pegs holding the tunnel down

More Trap Making – Step by Step

Wood & Other Materials

The American trapping websites, magazines and books are full of innovative ways to house and support the Bodygrip style of trap, including wooden tunnels and plastic buckets. Many of these can be adapted for use in the UK, provided that you remain within the terms of the **Spring Traps Approval Order.**

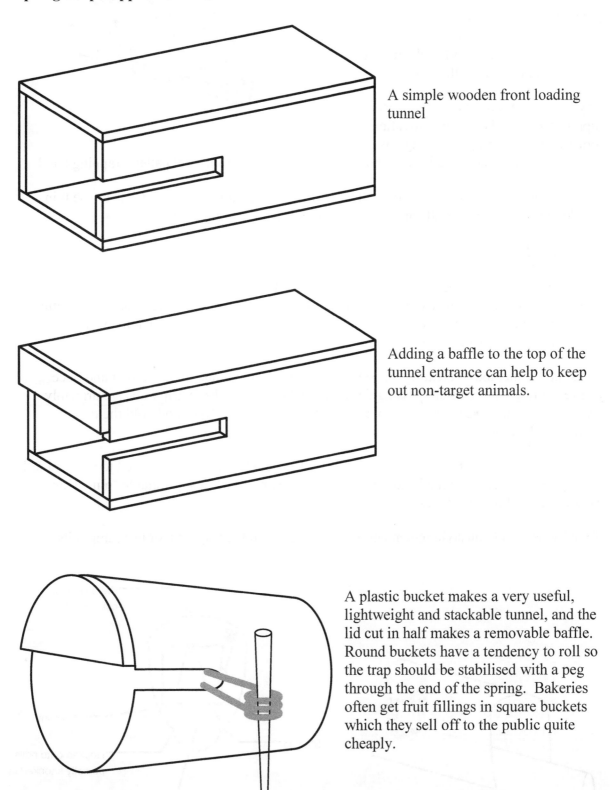

A simple wooden front loading tunnel

Adding a baffle to the top of the tunnel entrance can help to keep out non-target animals.

A plastic bucket makes a very useful, lightweight and stackable tunnel, and the lid cut in half makes a removable baffle. Round buckets have a tendency to roll so the trap should be stabilised with a peg through the end of the spring. Bakeries often get fruit fillings in square buckets which they sell off to the public quite cheaply.

The Supporting Cubby Tunnel

The ultimate tunnel for a Bodygrip trap is one which supports the trap as well as just protecting it from non-target species.

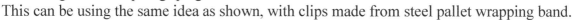

Cubby tunnels such as that shown here are made and sold commercially – made from wire mesh, plastic coated and fitted with spring steel clips to hold the trap at the top.

Any bodygrip tunnel can be converted to support the trap like this by providing something for the trap to grip against when set. This can be using the same idea as shown, with clips made from steel pallet wrapping band.

Alternatively wire hooks could be fitted to the roof of the trap. Another idea is to use thin wooden rails or wire 'U's attached to the tunnel sides and facing inwards.

The Rail Trap.

It's also worth mentioning a very useful set for both Fenn and Bodygrip style traps – the rail trap. It is particularly effective where squirrels regularly run along fence rails and on natural or artificial 'bridges' across streams or ditches. The latter are usually fallen trees or deliberately placed wooden planks.

The simplest method of creating this set is simply to fix the tunnel in place first and once you're confident animals are passing through it, add the trap. Bodygrip traps are arguably best suited to this type of set as a mount can be attached to the 'rail' and hold the trap in position. The tunnel ends can be 'fenced' by shaping the mesh.

Alternatively a complete rail trap unit can be built where the tunnel is attached to a baseboard slightly longer than the tunnel and this board can then be fixed to any suitable 'rail. This works well for both trap types.

If you're using a Fenn style remember to cut a slot to bed the trap into, or use jump rails.

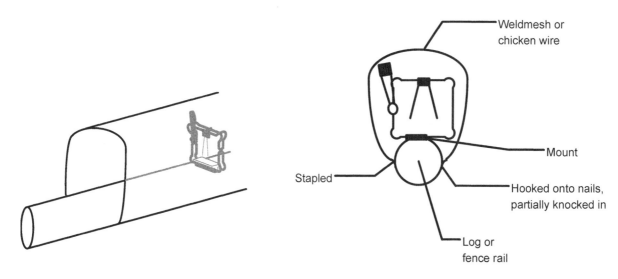

Using A Bodygrip Vertically

In the next chapter I write about the Kania Trap – probably the most effective and efficient trap you can currently buy for off the ground squirrel control. The downside is that they can seem a bit expensive – particularly if you need a lot or are likely to have them pinched !

This plan enables you to use a bodygrip trap in a similar way and had the working title of '*poor man's Kania trap*' during development. I created a few early prototypes of this set and have been testing it with the help of James Linari-Linholm of JLL Pest Control. This final design has been giving us reliable, clean catches and zero non-target species.

The basics of this design are simple. A bodygrip trap, when set tightly in a mount, is pretty much fixed there until it fires. It can be tilted upright on its side, on its edge or even upside down, as long at the dog is free to move and the weight of the trigger doesn't fire the trap.

A trap, fixed to a mount on a backboard, can be hung on the side of a tree, a fence, a wall or any other upright surface where a squirrel is seen to visit. However you still need to have a tunnel in place and in this case you need the tunnel to be fixed to the board so that it doesn't fall off. You also need to be able to get the trap set inside it.

Base Board

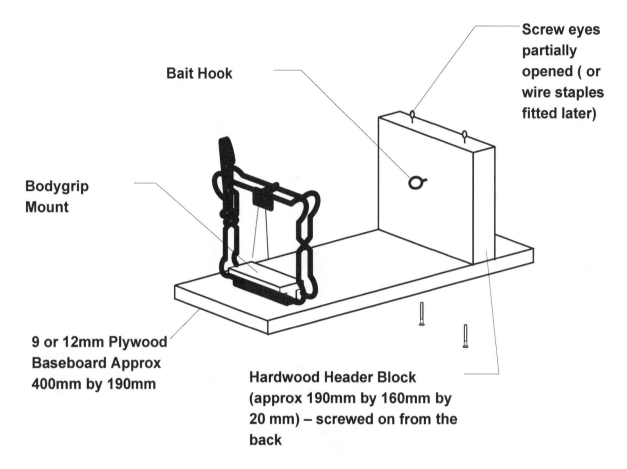

Bait Hook

Screw eyes partially opened (or wire staples fitted later)

Bodygrip Mount

9 or 12mm Plywood Baseboard Approx 400mm by 190mm

Hardwood Header Block (approx 190mm by 160mm by 20 mm) – screwed on from the back

The base board is just familiar 9mm or 12mm exterior grade plywood with a mount fixed roughly half way along. Attached to the board is a block of wood, preferably hardwood for longevity but softwood will do. The only reason for not using plywood here is that you're screwing into the edge of the block and the open edges of plywood don't suit this.

The block needs to be a little bigger than the frame of the bodygrip trap and should be fixed a little way in from one end of the board, to leave room for a hanging hole. In practice though, you could make the mounting holes anywhere on the backboard. The mesh tunnel will be hinged from the top edge of this block and I used small screw eyes to hold it in place. If you open them up a little with long nosed pliers you can 'hook' them over the mesh and then squeeze them closed again.

Make the surface of the board easy for the squirrel to climb up, by cutting rough grooves or covering it with a strip of thin mesh.

Fix a bodygrip mount to the backboard near to the open end. It needs to be slightly off the centre line of the baseboard because with the spring folded up, the trap is not quite in the middle.

The Tunnel

The most important thing to realise about the tunnel is that it's only fixed in one place – to the top of the block at one end. When you need to get inside the tunnel it lifts up and swings back up out of the way.

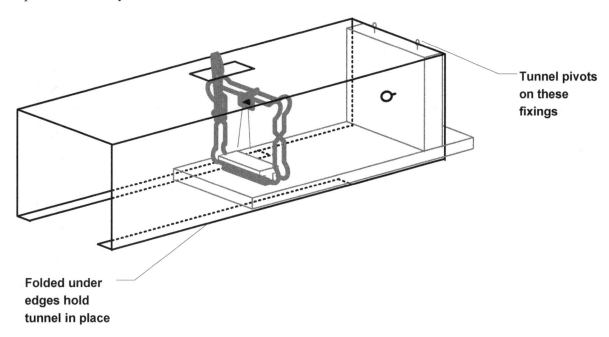

Tunnel pivots on these fixings

Folded under edges hold tunnel in place

The tunnel is mesh with the usual three sides but it also has an extra folded flap along the bottom edge of each side, for the lower ¾ of the tunnel length. When the tunnel is in place these flaps sit underneath the backboard and hold the tunnel in place. To raise the tunnel you simply pull the side out until the flaps are clear of the base board and then lift the tunnel upwards.

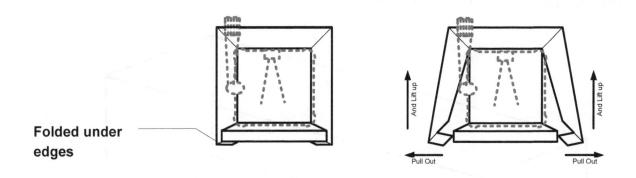

Folded under edges

Tunnel Template

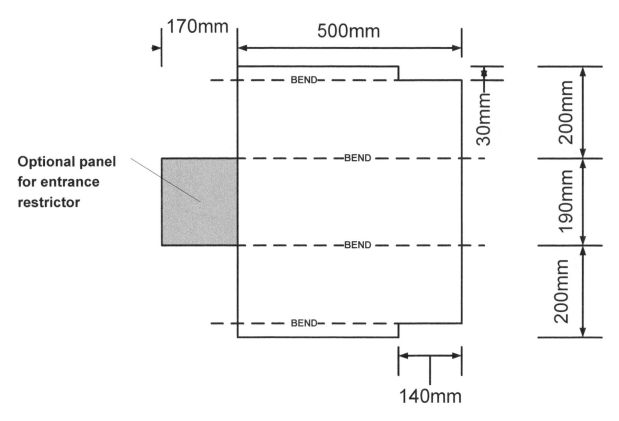

170mm | 500mm | 30mm | 200mm | 190mm | 200mm | 140mm

Optional panel for entrance restrictor

BEND

BEND

BEND

BEND

The mesh template is fairly straightforward, creating a 3 sided rectangular tunnel. If you want to build in some form of entrance restrictor just include the extra shaded panel, cut out the entrance shape that you want and fold this flap down over the open end of the tunnel. You can always add this later on as a single panel, clipped on if you decide that you need to.

The other key feature is the pair of narrow flaps that run most of the length of the tunnel sides. The upper section is cut away as this makes it easier to clip and unclip the tunnel from the base when it's swung up to access the trap.

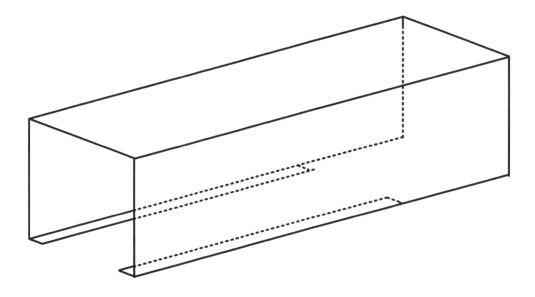

More Trap Making – Step by Step

Assembly

Take the trap you plan to use and set it in the holder that you've fixed to the board and fold the spring upwards. Personally at this point I'd put a cable tie around the trap so that it cannot fire while you're concentrating on the tunnel.

Without attaching it to the block, or clipping on the flaps, place the tunnel over the trap and look where the spring touches the tunnel. Mark the section that you need to cut away to allow the spring to poke though. Remove that section and then recheck. It's always better to go slowly and if necessary remove a bit at a time with regular rechecking.

When you're happy that the hole is large enough, hook the top edge of the tunnel onto the screw eyes on the block and squeeze them closed.

The tunnel should now pivot freely.

Take the two side of the tunnel, near the open end, and gently pull them apart. Take them under the backboard and release.

In order to exclude non target species the entrance to the mesh tunnel can be restricted.

In Use

All the testing that we've done has been using a Magnum 116 and we found that it is most effective when set 'light' – that is on the very first notch. Set any firmer and too often the squirrels were not caught as cleanly.

Bait is hung from the middle of the wooden block so that it is protected from the rain and from the attention of mice. Mice will still get in but we found that in early prototypes, which had mesh at the top, most mice seemed to approach the bait from above.

Having the baseboard stop shorter than the tunnel enables squirrels to climb up the surface of the tree trunk almost until they reach the trap.

Options & Alternatives

Long Baseboard Version

One alternative is to create the baseboard the same length as the tunnel. This can be a little more rigid but you need to make sure the backboard can be climbed.

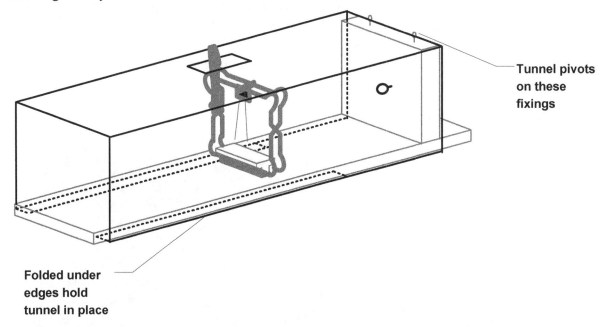

Tunnel pivots on these fixings

Folded under edges hold tunnel in place

You can make a similar vertical mount by fixing a supporting cubby to a backboard, provided that you can still set the trap with the board in place.

Rail trap

By adding extra flaps to the mesh tunnel template you can create a through tunnel, hinged from the baseboard at one end. This makes an great self contained rail trap.

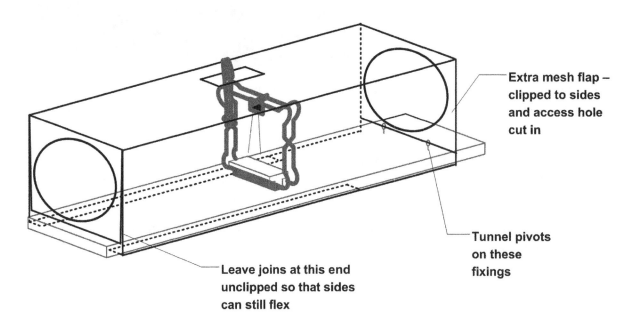

Extra mesh flap – clipped to sides and access hole cut in

Tunnel pivots on these fixings

Leave joins at this end unclipped so that sides can still flex

Chapter 4 – The Kania Trap

The Kania Trap is another trap designed for the wider range of quarry and the more relaxed rules of the Canadian and American markets. It is very powerful trap which ensures a quick, clean kill but is also quite capable of breaking your hand and so should be handled with care.

There are two models available, the 2000 and the 2500 both approved under the English Spring Traps Approval Order for use on grey squirrels, mink, stoats, weasels, rats, mice and other small ground vermin. In the UK it is most commonly used to control grey squirrels and to a lesser extent mink. It has the advantage of being easily mounted on trees, posts or walls so that it is out or reach from the ground – safe from accidents and free from interference.

The 2500 model is nothing more than the spring loaded killing bar, trigger mechanism and supporting framework. This provides a clear run through trap but must be built into an enclosed 'cubby' or tunnel to comply with UK law. The requirement for this kind of custom designed mounting is fairly rare and this book does not offer any designs for housing the 2500. In most cases a 2000 model will be quite suitable and any situation special enough to need the 2500 model would probably also have specific requirements for the housing.

The 2000 model is fitted with a box which covers the spring mechanism, protects the rear of the trap and serves as a bait holder. Under the Spring Trap Approval Order a suitable tunnel is also required on the entrance of the trap in order to minimise the chances of harming non-target species, particularly woodpeckers, when the trap is used on tree trunks.

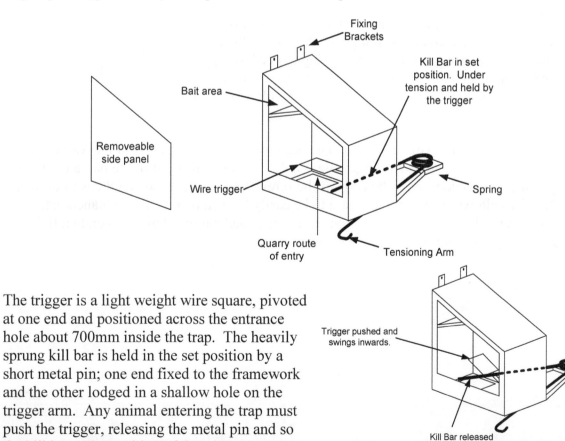

The trigger is a light weight wire square, pivoted at one end and positioned across the entrance hole about 700mm inside the trap. The heavily sprung kill bar is held in the set position by a short metal pin; one end fixed to the framework and the other lodged in a shallow hole on the trigger arm. Any animal entering the trap must push the trigger, releasing the metal pin and so the kill bar. The position of the trigger means that a head or chest strike is almost a certainty.

Preparation

In terms of tuning and tweaking there is nothing that needs to be done to improve the effectiveness of the Kania 2000 trap. However in their supplied state they are a bright and shiny silver colour making them very noticeable in use. A couple of coats of car spray paint, (dark green, black or brown), can make all the difference and render the traps almost invisible when installed on leafy trees. Painting the mounting board and tunnels in the same colour adds to the effect. Don't use house paint though as the smell lingers for months.

Mounting Board

The Kania 2000 does come with a pair of mounting brackets attached to the back of the rear box. These are riveted on and although fairly sturdy do not stand up to a lot of rough treatment. In theory these lugs could be used to fix the trap directly to the tree or wall and the tunnel attached separately. However in my experience it is far easier to permanently attach the trap to a Mounting Board, to which you can also fix the tunnel. This way you have a complete and integrated set up which you can simply hang on a nail or hook – much easier to move round from site to site. If the fixing brackets should come off the back of the trap, I simply drill out the rivets and use the same holes to bolt the box directly onto to the board. The casing is not that thick though so remember to use washers on the inside to prevent the bolt head enlarging the hole and pulling through.

My preference is for a light weight board of 12mm exterior grade plywood, 140mm wide and long enough for the tunnel, the trap plus an 80mm header to hang it from. It isn't going to need to support much weight and being hung from a tree most rain will quickly run off so marine plywood is unnecessary. If treated with a low odour wood preservative of a dark colour these will last for years.

I also favour a 'key-hole' style hanging hole cut into the middle of the Mounting Board near the top. The large hole is able to fit over the head of the nail and the slot then slides down over the body of the screw between the head and the wall or tree. This allows the Mounting Board to be easily hooked on or off a permanent nail or screw. This is a much more convenient arrangement than having to undo a fixing every time you want to move the trap.

Tunnels

The common misconception that you don't need to use a tunnel is probably because many of the marketing photos are from USA and Canada, where the legislation is more relaxed. In other cases tunnels have been removed to show how effectively and cleanly a squirrel had been caught. Also following changes to the STAO in 2012 there *may* be some circumstances where you don't need to use a tunnel but this is not clear and my advice is to use a tunnel in all cases.

The Spring Traps Approval Order does not give specific details on trap tunnels other than that they should be '*a natural or artificial tunnel which is suitable for minimising the chances of injuring or killing non-target species whilst not compromising the capture and killing of target species.*' In practice there is a choice between a mesh and a wooden tunnel both of which have their own merits.

Mesh Tunnels

Mesh tunnels are cheap, quick and easy to fit; a simple piece of medium gauge mesh bent into a curved or square tunnel and secured to the edges of the mounting board with wire staples. Shape the tunnel round the trap entrance to minimise any gaps and prevent access by small birds.

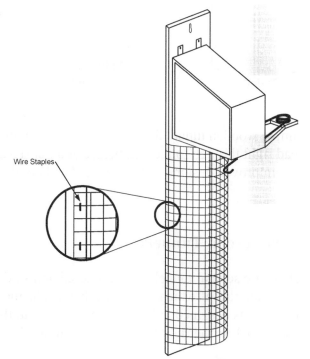

Wire Staples

The mesh provides an easy and comfortable climbing surface. Any catches are clearly visible from the ground or even from a distance using binoculars, reducing the time required to manage a large number of traps deployed over a wide area.

However with increasing public access to even the remotest areas of the countryside, it may not be appropriate to have such a visible indicator of success.

In order to comply with UK law I would recommend this sort of tunnel as the <u>minimum</u> you need to use.

Wooden Tunnels

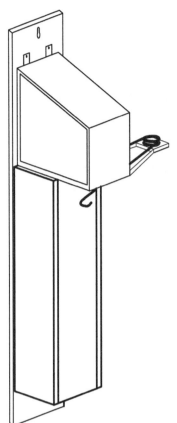

An alternative is to use a simple wooden tunnel firmly fixed to the mounting board. It's easy to make using the same material as for the mounting board and gives a much more professional and long lasting set up.

Wooden tunnels also have a number of other advantages. Any catches are hidden from view and from scavenging crows, making it much more discreet and public friendly. A visual check of the trap is still quite practical but relies on looking at the trap spring and the position of the Kill Bar – either set or fired.

Dark enclosed tunnels are also likely to be less attractive to birds and so reduce the chances of catching any by accident. Tunnel length is a tricky issue. The shorter the tunnel is the more likely that the squirrels will enter, but it's also the more likely that non-target species will enter too.

Personally I wouldn't use anything shorter than 230mm. If you make it long and find that it's not catching, it's relatively easy to cut the length down.

The plan on the next few pages shows you how to make and fit a simple wooden tunnel for a Kania trap. As with all the chapters though, I'd encourage you to read right through to the end before you get started. In the Options and Variations there are few improved designs that you might feel comfortable jumping to straight away.

Commercial Tunnels

There are several tunnels manufactured and sold commercially for use with the Kania trap, two examples of which are shown here. The mesh version on the left is sold by Magnum Trap Co, is designed to be mounted directly to the tree and can be 'stacked' for easier storage. The tunnel on the right has an integral mounting board and is sold by Kilgerm.

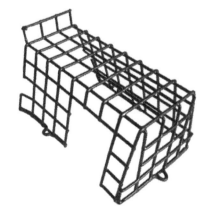
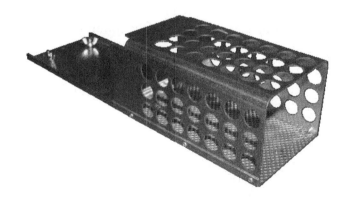

Plan for a Wooden Kania Tunnel

1 Cut two sides and a top from 9mm or 12mm exterior grade plywood and to the sizes shown in the diagram. The shortest that the tunnel should be is 230mm and it can be longer, but too long and the squirrels may be reluctant to use it. The top should always be 15mm longer than the sides so that it fits into the alcove on the front of the trap.

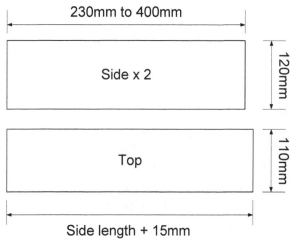

You will also need two short 5mm screws and 8 or 10 oval wire nails 20 or 25mm long.

2 Take one Side and mark a line about 5mm in from one of the long edges. Take 4 or 5 nails, and at roughly equal intervals start the nails off along the marked line.

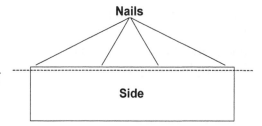

3 Repeat for the other Side piece.

4 Assemble the tunnel by nailing the two sides onto the edge of the tunnel Top. Make sure that the ends of the Side and Top are all flush at one end. The Top should stick out 15mm at the other end.

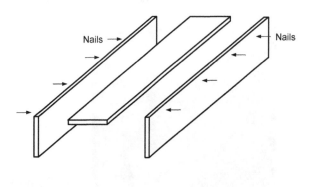

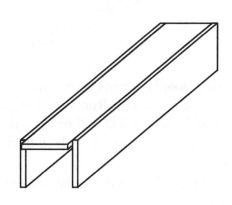

5 The next step is to fit the tunnel to the Mounting Board. In some ways this is easier to do if the Kania itself is not yet attached as there is less weight to handle but it's always worth doing a 'dry' test at this stage.

6 Place the Kania onto the Mounting Board in the position you plan to fix it – central across the board and about 100 to 150mm down from the top. If you've already drilled the hanging hole in the Mounting Board make sure that is at the right end !

7   Place the tunnel onto the board, with the 'lip' of the top next to the Kania. Holding the trap in place, slide the tunnel so that it locates into the front of the trap casing.
It won't be a tight fit but should neatly block any access from the tunnel sides.

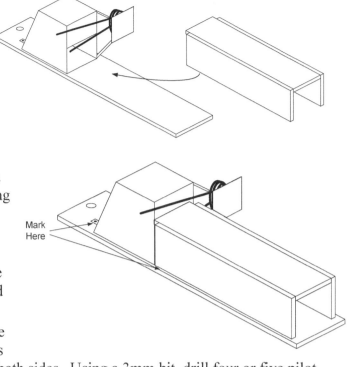

8   Using a pencil, mark the Mounting Board where the holes of the Kania fixing brackets are. Also draw along the outside edges of the tunnel for the full length. Remove the Kania trap and the tunnel.

9   Use a bradawl or large nail to make starter holes at these points marked for the fixing brackets

Mark
Here

10 Measure approximately 5mm inside the lines marked at the tunnel edges and mark another line. Do this on both sides. Using a 3mm bit, drill four or five pilot holes right through the Mounting board

Marked Lines &
points

Pilot Holes

11 Turn the Mounting Board over and start nails in the holes you have just made. Run a bead of glue along the edges of the tunnel that will be in contact with the board and carefully reposition the tunnel between the marked lines.

12 Gently hammer in the nails and check that the tunnel is correctly positioned.

13 Finally replace the Kania trap on the mounting board. Ensure that it correctly aligns with the tunnel and fix it into place using a screw in each of the fixing brackets.

Options and Variations

Internal Climbing Surface

There is no doubt that the grey squirrel has an outstanding ability to climb, however almost everything in the wild has a relatively rough surface allowing the feet and claws to get a grip. I can't help feeling that an artificial tunnel of smooth, planed wood is not quite so easy. Although it might be completely unnecessary I always make a point of improving the climbing surface as I want to make it as easy as possible to reach the trap.

Suitable methods, applied to the Mounting board or _inside_ of the tunnel, include:

- Cutting shallow grooves with a saw, router or even a sharp knife.

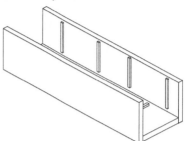

- Attaching a narrow strip of light weight mesh.

- Nailing or gluing on thin strips of wood at intervals.

Don't make it too complicated though or you may have trouble removing your catch.

Hinged Tunnel

You may prefer to be able to easily remove the wooden tunnel in case you get a catch that is difficult to remove.

Hinging the tunnel is one option although a hasp and staple should be used so that the tunnel can be locked closed to prevent any accidents. An alternative is to split the tunnel into two sections and only hinge the lower half.

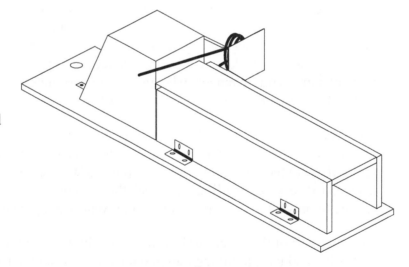

Side Entry Tunnel

Many experts also believe that using a tunnel with an entrance on the side can reduce the risk to birds like the treecreeper, nuthatch and particularly woodpeckers which regularly travel up the trunks of trees looking for food.

Side entry tunnels should be made shorter.

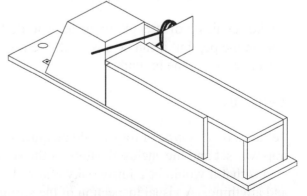

Mounting Board Modification

As with the vertical mount bodygrip in the last chapter– sometimes the best climbing surface is the tree you're mounting the trap onto. As long as you leave yourself a means to attach the tunnel don't be afraid to change the design or length of the Mounting Board to take advantage of that.

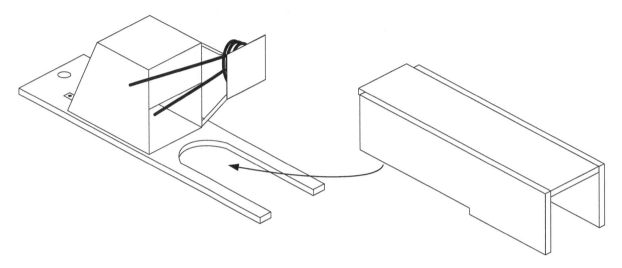

Lofting socket

I have already described how the Mounting Board arrangement, with a 'keyhole' hanging hole, makes it very easy to install and remove a Kania trap in any number of sites where you have put a suitable hanging peg. If they are located high up though, this still leaves the tiresome business of taking some sort of ladder with you when you check or move the traps. I know of some wildlife rangers who are able to park their vehicle underneath and climb on the roof rack to reach the traps, but this wouldn't work for most of us.

One simple solution is to make the Mounting Board a little wider and add a Lofting Socket next to the tunnel. This is nothing more than a piece of tube blocked at the top end and very firmly fixed to the board. I have used a piece of kitchen waste pipe with a block of wood screwed to the Mounting Board to block the top but a metal tube is better. The pipe needs to be long to prevent the set up twisting – the weaker the pipe the longer it needs to be.

The other part of the apparatus is a stout pole, like a broom handle, that can be inserted into the Socket and used to lift the trap into the air and onto the hanging peg.

It takes a fair bit of strength in the arms to do this and control the wobble enough to hang the trap on the peg but it can be a very efficient way of servicing traps placed out of reach of a person stood on the ground.

Telltales

Telltales on this type of trap would be quite fiddly to do. They need to be applied whilst the trap was set and the enclosed nature of the set up, combined with the power of the trap spring, means that it would be a fairly risky affair. Luckily with an exterior spring there is no need to add anything. A visual inspection of the spring position will immediately tell you if the trap has fired. If you want a more visible indicator fix a loop of Forestry Tape around the spring when it's set. When the spring fires the loop will be ripped open and fall away.

In Use

<u>This is a killing trap.</u>
<u>Do not use it in any area where there is a possibility that red squirrels are present.</u>

<u>If there is likely to be any public access or children in the area set it high up, out of reach.</u>

Baiting

Baiting the trap is the first step. In my opinion it is good practice to minimise any time that your fingers are inside the housing once the trap has been set, so I do everything I can beforehand.

The top corner of the housing is a little bait compartment which is separated from the rest of the housing by a piece of wire mesh. The main bait should be placed in here. Peanuts work very well as a bait for grey squirrels and I usually smear a little peanut butter on the mesh. I also smear just a touch on the entrance to the tunnel as well where the scent catches on the wind more easily.

Be prepared to try different baits if you have no success. Think about what food is readily available in the area, how much of it there is and how active the animals are. You're not likely to have much success using apples as bait in an orchard in the autumn.

Also refresh the bait frequently. It's very easy to think of the bait as everlasting because the target animals are killed before they reach it, but heat, moisture, snails and insects will all take their toll. You'd be surprised how quickly a tasty treat can become an odourless, unappetising pile of dust or goo – or even disappear completely.

If trapping a new area with a high squirrel population it is important to 'pre-bait' the area. That is running the trap baited but unset for a few days or even a couple of weeks. Remove the mesh grill on the bait compartment as it is important that the squirrels can actually reach and take the bait and this will establish the trap as a reliable feeding point in their mind. Experience suggests that once trapping begins, squirrels familiar with a trap in this way are less likely to be put off by seeing any kills in the trap.

Placement

The most effective deployment of this trap is to place it on trees, walls or garden structures where squirrels are active. Be prepared to move it about and for best results have a variety of permanent hanging points dotted around your target area. If you stop catching in one place move the trap to another spot.

The trap needs to be stable when in use as sudden movement or rocking can deter the squirrels. Having the trap and tunnel fixed to a Mounting Board helps but there are other things you can do if you have problems. A simple bungee cord placed near the bottom of the Board and going round the tunnel and tree is a quick way to add stability. Another option is to make two hanging holes in the top of Mounting Board instead of one as I have shown – hanging on a pair of nails stops the trap swinging.

Setting

Before doing anything with a Kania Trap, make sure that it is not set and keep your hand away from the trap entrance at all times. It could break your hand, let alone your fingers.

Never try to set or unset the trap while it is in place on a tree or building. It's possible that you will fall off and the torque of the spring may pull the trap off its mountings.

1. Place the trap on the ground or on a firm surface. Hold the trap housing down firmly with your left hand and un-hook the outer spring with your other hand. The outer spring is located just above the trap entrance and hooked under a small metal lip.

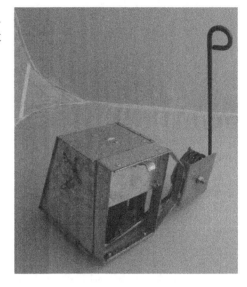

2. Slide the catch to release the side panel and remove it. This gives you access to the area behind the kill bar where you can set and bait the trap. There is a small compartment separated from the rest of the trap compartment by a strip of mesh. The compartment is intended for loose bait such as nuts but baits like peanut butter can be smeared anywhere within the trap compartment.

3. Push the spring right back so that the strike bar, (the internal part of the spring) is against the top of the trap. Make sure that the *dog* is not pinned against the casing. (The 'dog' is the heavy wire that hangs down from just above the trap entrance).

4. Now lift the dog upwards and notch the end of it into the shallow hole in the front of the trigger arm. The trap is now primed but not finally set or 'cocked'. When the spring is tensioned again the dog will hold the strike bar in place and poised to be released.

5. Put the side panel back on and lock it in place.

6. Place the trap back onto a firm surface and again holding the trap with your left hand, push the outer spring down and re-hook it under the small metal lip.

Your trap is now FULLY SET.

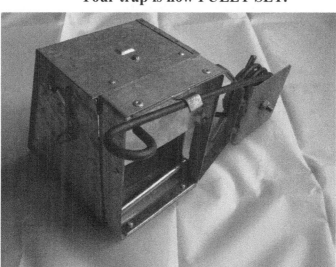

Releasing the Trap

Quite often you will want to release the spring and 'un-set' the trap while you move it to a new location or refresh the bait. Unhooking the tensioning spring as you did to set the trap puts it into a harmless state.

If you want to demonstrate or test fire the trap always use a soft material such as a rolled up newspaper to fire the spring. Never use a hard object like a stick as this will damage the trap and the stick may shatter causing flying debris. Even a small bend in the killing bar will great a gap and reduce the effectiveness of trap.

Chapter 5 – Other Approved Traps

The Spring Traps Approval Order includes quite a large number of traps and the list is regularly amended as new traps are added and some of the older ones are removed. In this chapter I have covered a few of the other traps which are slightly less popular but still fairly well known.

Imbra & Juby

The Imbra trap (on the left), was another of the traps patented as part of the rush to find replacements for the gin trap. Primarily a rabbit trap, the Imbra was produced in two versions (Mk 1 and Mk 2) and is still widely regarded as an excellent trap for use in the entrances to rabbit burrows. As you can see from the photos below, the Juby trap (on the right) has a very similar jaw action and was another excellent rabbit trap.

Collarum

The Collarum could perhaps be described as an automated snare but it's a bit more than that. It is canine-specific because of the trigger mechanism, which requires a pull action rather than the push/depress mechanism usually employed by traps. This goes a long way towards eliminating catches of animals outside the dog 'family'. The English approved version also features a Relax-a-lock cable and adjustable stop to ensure a 'friendly' capture – so even if a pet is caught there is no permanent harm done.

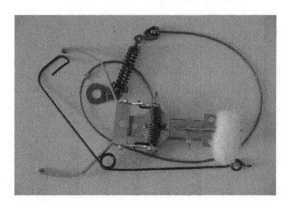

WCS Tube Trap

This very powerful trap is relatively new to the UK and completely self contained, making it very safe and simple to use. It needs no additional tunnels or mountings and is approved for rats through to mink.

As with any trap care must be taken to exclude non-target species. This can be done using rods pushed through the holes at the tube ends or with special plastic end caps. The end caps can also be used to create a 'blind' set with the tube sealed and baited at one end.

Setting the Trap

As this trap will be unfamiliar to many people, I have included some basic instructions on how it should be set – based on those supplied by the manufacturer.

1. Place the trap on a flat piece of ground with the trigger mechanism on the ground facing away from you and push the safety catch and the trigger away from you.

2. Place the palms of your hands on the top of the Tube Trap and put your thumbs on the corners of the double torsion spring.

3. Check that the safety catch and trigger catch are away from you and then push the spring bar down to the trigger mechanism.

4. Hold the spring bar down and flick the safety catch towards you to engage onto the bar.

   If you relax your grip the spring bar will rise slightly but cannot spring back because it is held by the safety catch.

5. Taking care not to disengage the safety, push the spring bar down again and then, using your forefinger, lift the trigger catch over the spring bar and engage it below the trigger plate (rear of floor pan).

6. Adjust the trigger catch so that it is as close to the edge of the trigger as possible. This makes for a 'fine' set, needing little weight on the trigger floor pan to set off the trap. When achieved the floor pan will be level with, or slightly lower than, the killing bars inside the tube.

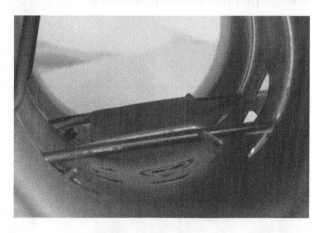

7. Place the trap in position and secure it to the ground using the holes in the ends of the tube. Traps need to be stable. Animals are reluctant to enter unstable traps. Camouflage it using local materials and where necessary reduce the openings to make entry specific for your intended target species. Finally remove the safety catch.

The DOC Trap

Taking its name from the New Zealand *Department of Conservation* who helped develop it, this is a range of 3 very powerful and humane traps. Although still quite slow to become popular in the UK, the DOC 150 is the best all round model for UK species.

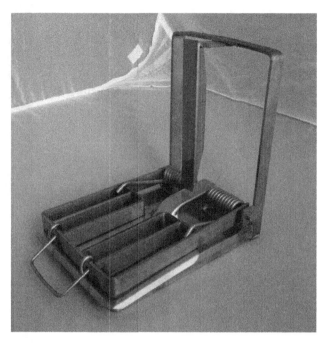

One limitation is that until recently the trap could only be used in a special wooden housing made and shipped from New Zealand – making an already quite expensive trap completely unaffordable. However changes in the 2012 Spring Traps Approval Order now permits housings to be made locally, to the Department Of Conservation design and standards.

These pictures show the DOC 200 – the slightly larger and more powerful trap. **In these pictures the trap is shown unset.**

Chapter 6 - Mole Traps

There are many different designs of mole trap on the market and many more that have been tried and used over the centuries. Small Ground Vermin Traps Order 1958 exempts spring traps of a kind commonly used for catching moles in their runs. Getting the most from your traps and the art of mole trapping is covered in great detail by Wayne Walton in his DVD 'Professional Mole Control' (see Further Resources). This chapter is limited to the basics of the most popular types of trap in use today.

Half Barrel Mole Traps

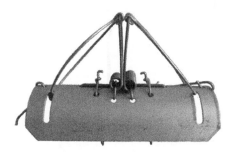

These are a very popular and effective mole trap, often referred to as 'Duffus' after the supplier most commonly associated with this design. Part of the attraction of these traps is that they are double ended and so capable of catching two moles in a single setting – one from each direction. This not just a theoretical possibility but is a quite common occurrence for professional mole catchers.

Fine Tuning

There are many different suppliers of this design and the finished quality of the traps can vary enormously. In some cases you may find that some of the adjustments recommended here have already been applied during manufacture.

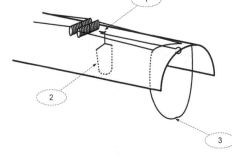

Adjustment 1 – Trigger release

This is the most delicate but most important area that needs to be checked and adjusted.

By looking at the trigger side-on you can see how the mechanism works. The firing of the trap relies on the mole pushing the lower part of the trigger forwards with its head or snout. This causes the top of the trigger to pivot the other way, allowing the retaining bar to slip off and release the spring.

Clearly if this requires the mole to push with a lot of force or to move the trigger a large distance then it increases the chance of the mole sensing that something is not quite right. If this happens he or she will back out of the trap and fill it with earth.

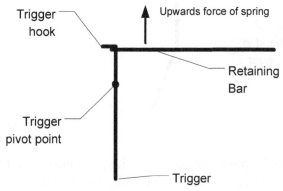

Trigger hook

Upwards force of spring

Retaining Bar

Trigger pivot point

Trigger

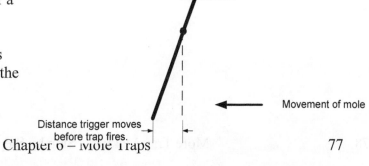

Movement of mole

Distance trigger moves before trap fires.

By bending the top of the trigger into a slightly upwards angle, and if necessary shortening the same section, the trap can be made to fire earlier and require much less force to set it off. This bend only needs to be very slight and has been exaggerated in the diagrams below to make the point clear. In practice make only a small adjustment and test before adjusting more if necessary.

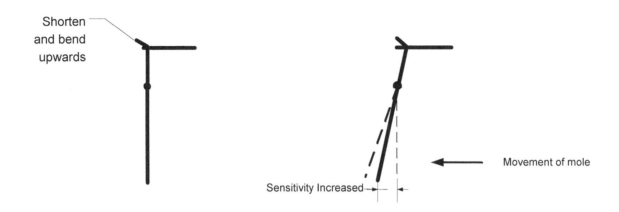

Adjustment 2 – Trigger shape

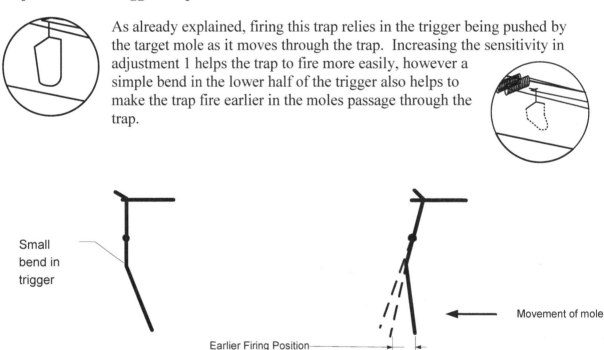

As already explained, firing this trap relies in the trigger being pushed by the target mole as it moves through the trap. Increasing the sensitivity in adjustment 1 helps the trap to fire more easily, however a simple bend in the lower half of the trigger also helps to make the trap fire earlier in the moles passage through the trap.

This is important because it helps to ensure that the loop of the trap catches the mole around the chest area giving a virtually instant kill. A late triggering of the trap can lead to a mole being caught round the middle or hind quarters which is not immediately fatal.

Adjustment 3 – Catching Loop Shape

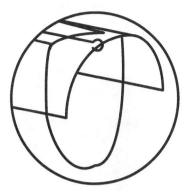

The final adjustment relates more to the trap going undetected, rather than its action. Many half barrel traps are manufactured with fully curved catching loops. If the loop shape is too narrow it can lead to the sides sticking out at the bottom of the tunnel and being detected by the mole.

Two small bends either side of the loop will flatten the bottom and broaden the loop slightly, making it a better fit for the tunnel shape.

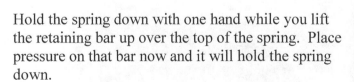

How to Set

Hold the trap in one hand and ensure that the retaining bar, attached to the very end of the trap, is hanging free.

While you're setting the trap it is important that you keep your fingers away from the end of the trap and out of the trap loops.

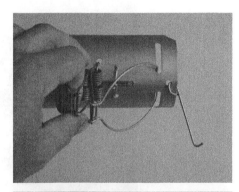

Gripping the edges of the trap with your finger, use your thumbs to press down one of the spring loops.

Hold the spring down with one hand while you lift the retaining bar up over the top of the spring. Place pressure on that bar now and it will hold the spring down.

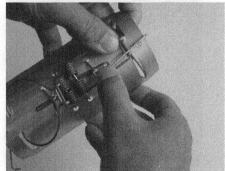

The task now is to lock the end of the retaining bar under the hook at the top of the trigger.

Holding the retaining bar in place, use your fingers on the underside of the trap to manoeuvre the trigger gently until the two hooks fit together. Gently release pressure on the retaining bar until the force of the spring locks the two hooks together.

 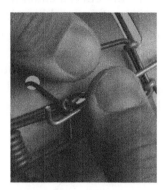 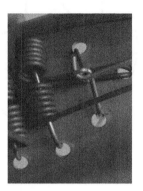

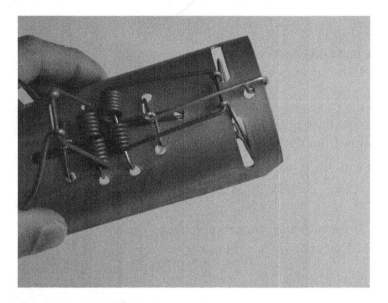

Repeat the process to set the trap at the other end.

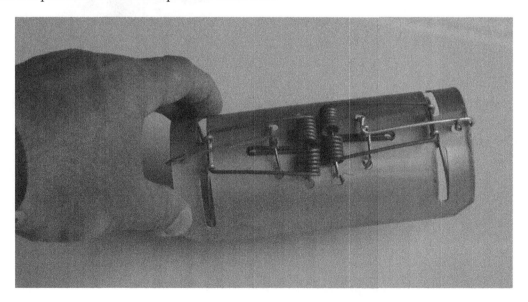

Mole Trapping Accessories

There are some basic tools that you'll need, some of which you'll probably have available:

- A trowel or small spade to dig out the hole for placing the trap.

- An old knife for cutting through the turf on lawns or pasture. This is particularly useful if you're using a trowel and helps to give you neat clean hole on the surface.

- Markers – your mole traps will be underground so you need markers on the surface to be able to locate them again. Typical markers are wire 'pegs' with string or tape on the end, wooden pegs, feathers, spray paint or even GPS waypoints. Depending where you are trapping your markers may need to be discreet to minimise interference.

- Gloves - these aren't crucial and many mole catchers work bare handed. Clean hands though are essential! Animal or chemical smells on your hands or traps will keep moles away from your traps when they are in the ground.

There are other tools which are specific to mole trapping that you'll need to buy or make.

- **Mole Probe**
  A probe is an essential tool for locating mole runs under ground. The probe is firmly and steadily pushed into the ground and if it hits a tunnel there is a distinct feeling of the soil 'giving way' as the probe breaks through. Most probes have a slightly bulbous end which exaggerates this effect. Once a run is found the probe can be used to find the direction of the run and identify a suitable spot to place a trap.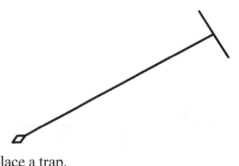

- **Tunnel Clearer**
  A piece of high tensile wire bent into a long 'U' shape and attached to a wooden handle. This device is extremely useful for removing debris which has been pushed back into the tunnels when the hole was being dug. The loop 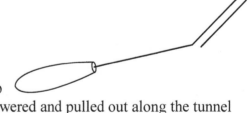 is pushed into the top half of the tunnel, then lowered and pulled out along the tunnel floor, dragging any debris into the open where it can be removed.

- **Tunnel Smoother**
  Even after you have removed as much of the debris as you can from the ends of the tunnel, it will still not be a smooth and clear as the rest of the mole's run. This change in condition can be enough to alert the mole that something is not quite right and to cause him to back fill your trap. By cutting down the wooden handle of an old spade, you can make a very useful device that can be used to flatten and smooth the inside of the the tunnel. Some people use the handle of the probe to do this, although it can be a bit too thin.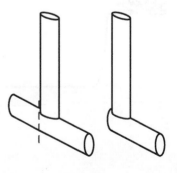

How to place the trap

Placing a mole trap successfully is a skill. If done correctly the trap will be undetectable by a mole until it fires. Common mistakes include:

- The trap being left too loose so that it moves when the trigger is pushed

- Leaving debris in the tunnel.

The ideal site for a trap is on a straight section of tunnel, preferably level, without branches and away from any mole hills.

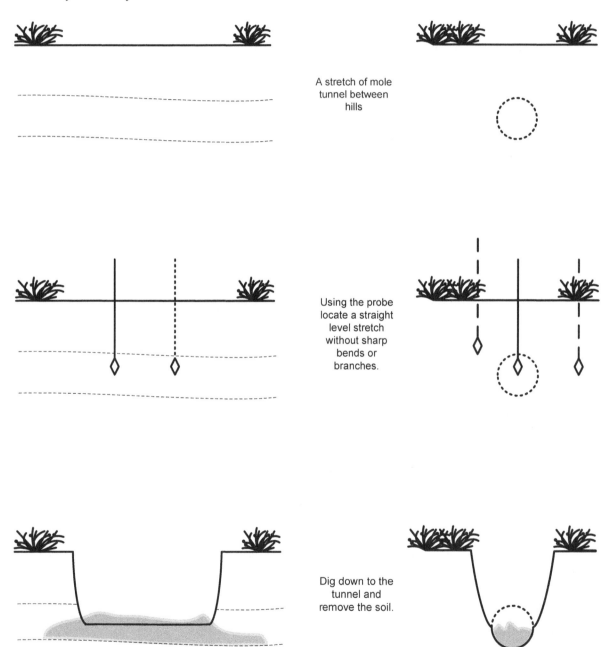

A stretch of mole tunnel between hills

Using the probe locate a straight level stretch without sharp bends or branches.

Dig down to the tunnel and remove the soil.

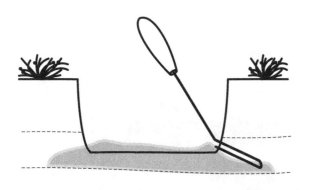

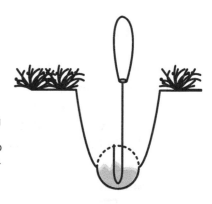

Remove all debris including any that has been pushed up the tunnel ends.

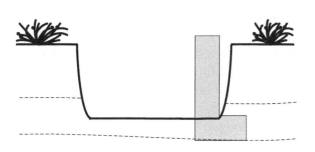

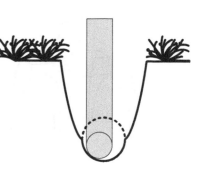

Use the probe handle or tool to smooth and flatten the bottom of the tunnel.

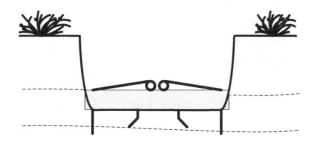

Place the trap firmly in the tunnel, with the loops pushed below the floor of the tunnel.

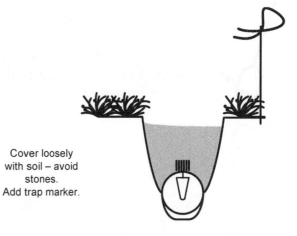

Cover loosely with soil – avoid stones. Add trap marker.

Chapter 6 – Mole Traps

Scissor Traps

The 'scissor' type is another very popular style of mole trap and the sort most often seen in hardware and countryside shops. There are many different variations of this trap available but all work in the same basic way.

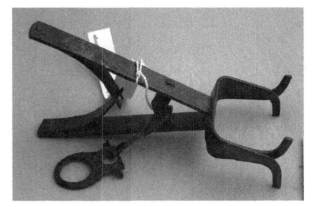

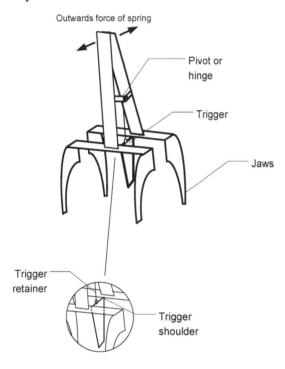

The trap has two pairs of spring loaded jaws which when sprung work in a scissor action to catch and crush the mole. When set the jaws are propped apart by a simple trigger – a piece of metal placed between the arms of the trap and held there by the force of the spring. The lower part of the trigger hangs down to block the path of any mole that passes through the trap. If the trigger is dislodged the jaws close and the mole is caught. These traps are able to catch a single mole travelling from either direction.

The only tuning required on these traps is carried out on the trigger piece itself.

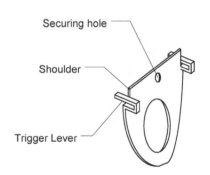

Preparation

Adjustment 1 – Trigger Attachment

On some brands of scissor trap the trigger is attached to the rest of the trap using a short length of straight wire with a loop at either end. Replace this wire linkage with a length of soft and flexible cord to increase the freedom and range of movement in the trigger.

Adjustment 2 – Trigger Release

Just as with the the half-barrel traps, this adjustment is all about increasing the sensitivity of the trigger mechanism. In scissor traps the trigger is held by the sprung jaws gripping the shoulders of the trigger. The trigger moves when pushed by the mole and the trigger lever pushes the trigger out from between the jaws.

The problem with most scissor traps, as they are manufactured, is that the trigger has to be pushed quite a long way before it slips out and fires the trap. There are two very easy methods improve this.

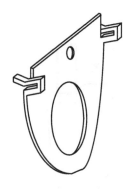

Option A

Using a pair a pliers bend the Trigger Lever upwards on both sides so that rather than being flat, it forms a shallow 'V'. This results in the trigger sitting lower when set and with less movement needed.

Before adjustment

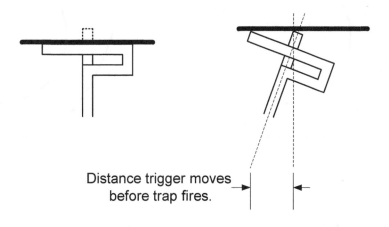

Distance trigger moves before trap fires.

After adjustment

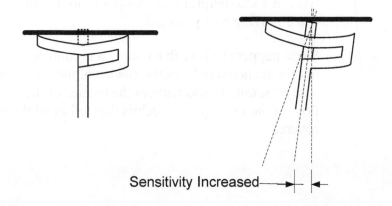

Sensitivity Increased

Option B

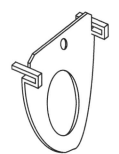

You can achieve the same effect by slightly filing down the shoulders of the trigger. Take a small amount off the corner on each side but don't do too much at a time and be careful to keep testing. Unlike option A, you can't bend this back if you've take too much off.

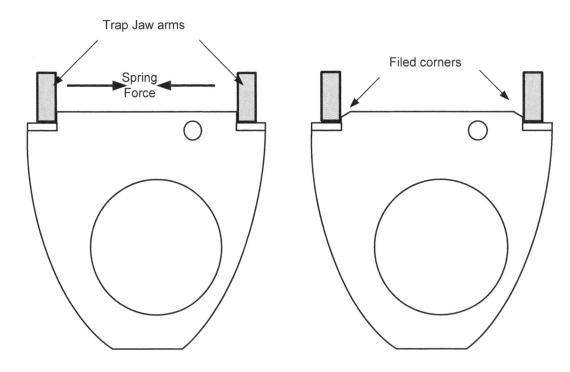

Trap Jaw arms

Spring Force

Filed corners

Adjustment 3 – Trigger Cutaway

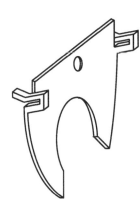

This last adjustment is less important than the others but is worth trying on a few of your traps. One of the tricks of professional mole trapping is to have a variety of traps that you can use according to soil type. It's also helpful to have options to try when faced with a mole that's proving tricky to catch.

Some trappers believe that cutting a section out of the bottom of the trigger as shown reduces the chance of the mole detecting the trigger with its snout. It also reduces the chance of the trigger catching on the floor of the tunnel or any debris that fell in while the trap was being covered.

How to Set

These instructions show a FENN scissor mole trap, but the method is common to all of this type.

Squeeze the handles of the trap together to fully open the jaws.

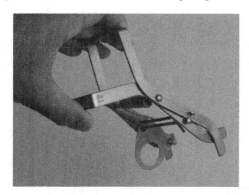 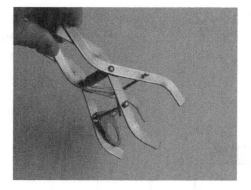

Take the trigger and locate it across the mouth of the trap, so that the shoulder rests against the retaining bar.

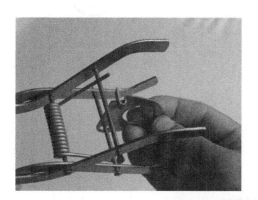 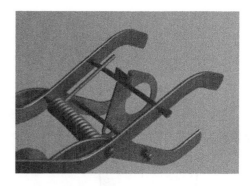

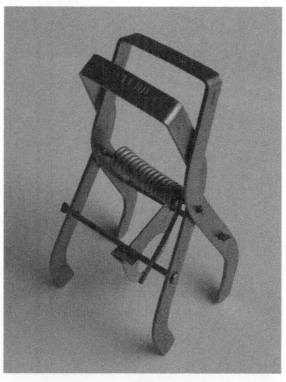

How to place the trap

Locate, dig and clean the runs as described above for the half-barrel trap. The scissor traps are usually shorter (i.e. cover a shorter section), so make sure that you only uncover as much tunnel as you need to.

Because the scissor traps doesn't have the solid cover that the Half Barrel traps has, you cannot simply fill the hole with loose soil or it will fall through into the tunnel. Once the trap is in place carefully block the large openings using sections of turf or , if the soil is clay like, by squeeing soil together to create firm clumps.

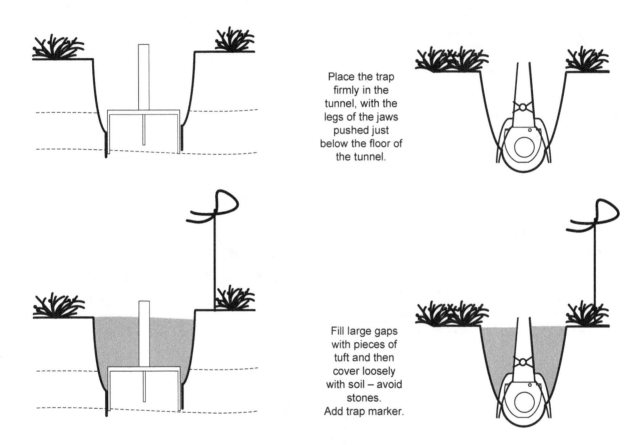

Place the trap firmly in the tunnel, with the legs of the jaws pushed just below the floor of the tunnel.

Fill large gaps with pieces of tuft and then cover loosely with soil – avoid stones. Add trap marker.

Talpex Style

The talpex mole trap and those of a similar style are becoming very popular amongst professional mole catchers. These generally require no adjustment and have a trigger mechanism which works in a completely different way to most common mole traps.

Rather than relying on the mole pushing the trigger horizontally, this trap is triggered by the natural upwards movement that a mole makes when digging.

Instead of ensuring a clean and empty tunnel when placing the trap, the space below the trap should be filled with fine soil to simulate a tunnel collapse. This is a frequent occurance in mole tunnels, particularly when there are cattle in the field above. It is the action of the mole clearing the tunnel that fires the trap.

How to Set

Squeeze the top handles of the trap together so that the Retaining Bar hangs down towards the trigger.

Using you other hand tilt the trigger so that the end of the Retaining Bar fits into the hole on the short side of the trigger.

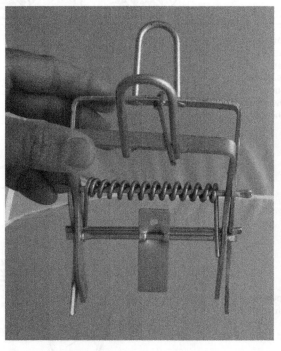
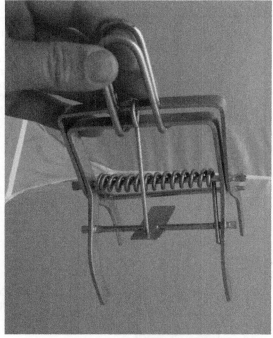

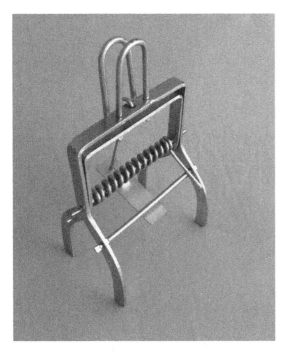

When set, the trigger will hold the Retaining Bar in place, which in turn holds the two handles together against the force of the spring.

When placing the trap make sure that there is enough room for the Retaining Bar to swing upwards when the trap fires. If the tunnel is too narrow cut a small 'V' in the side wall to accomodate the movement of the bar.

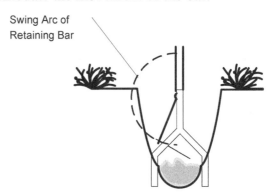

Swing Arc of
Retaining Bar

How to place the trap

Locate, dig and clean the runs as described earlier. The scissor traps are usually shorter so make sure that you only remove as much as you need to.

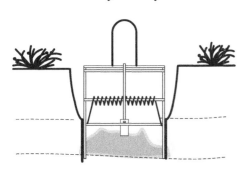

Place the trap firmly in the tunnel, with the legs of the jaws pushed just below the floor of the tunnel.

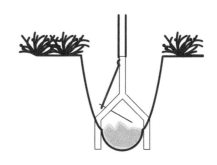

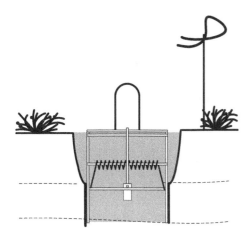

Cover **loosely** with soil – avoid stones. Add trap marker.

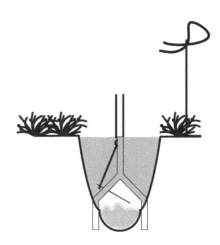

NoMol

The NoMol is an example of a trap that is inserted along the tunnel, rather than used at the point you break through.   It has the advantage of being completely below ground which makes it ideal where there is a risk of traps being interfered with or causing a nuisance.   It is based on a design 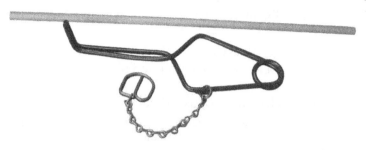 popular in France for many years, where it was usually made of copper. The NoMol brand is an American made version, made from modern materials and zinc coated.

The only adjustment required is to check that the connection between the trigger and the chain is squeezed tightly closed. This won't affect the operation of the trap but to lose a trigger in the middle of mole trapping can be frustrating.

How to Set

The trap is set by squeezing together the two sides of the trap and inserting the shaped wire trigger between the front prongs. This trigger keeps them wide enough apart for the mole to get through between the shaped ends. When the trigger is dislodged by the snout of the mole it springs away allowing the the prongs to spring closed - killing the mole.

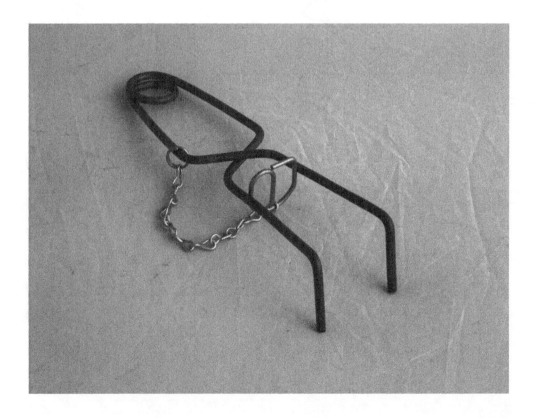

How to place the trap

Locate, dig and clean the runs as described previously.

The set trap is placed into the tunnel with the two shaped prongs pointing downwards. Be careful not to disturb the run too much or to push the prongs deep into the tunnel floor.

The wooden stick is pushed down through the loop at the end of the trap to hold it in position and prevent the trap being pushed along the tunnel by the mole.

When filling in the hole, use lumps of soil or turf to cover the traps so that loose soil does not spill into the tunnel.

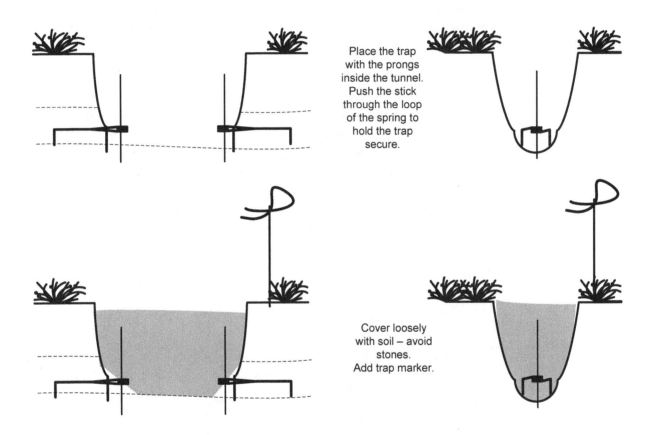

Place the trap with the prongs inside the tunnel. Push the stick through the loop of the spring to hold the trap secure.

Cover loosely with soil – avoid stones. Add trap marker.

Where to place your traps

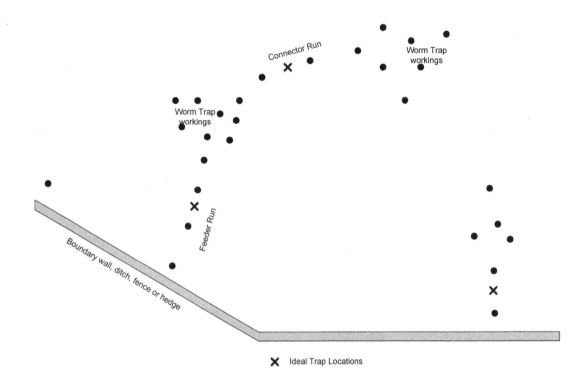

Moles feed mostly on worms and part of the function of the mole tunnels is to collect worms that burrow through the sides or top. Moles will select a small area and criss-cross it with many short tunnels of different depths to create what Wayne Walton calls a 'worm trap'. These areas are very complex and almost impossible to trap.

These concentrated networks enable a mole to eat a large number of worms fairly quickly and can soon exhaust the immediate supply of worms. The mole may simply extend the worm trap a little every day, throwing up one of two new hills or create a new set of workings a little way off.

The trick to successful trap placement is to target the Feeder Runs, the simple direct tunnels which connect the Worm Trap workings to each other, or to the main runs which usually follow a boundary hedge or wall.

More Trap Making – Step by Step

SECTION 2

TRAP MAKING PROJECTS

Traps & Tools to Make

Chapter 7 – The Mesh Bender

The first plan in this section is not a trap – but it's something that will be very useful in many trap making projects. In Trap Making Step by Step I discussed the use of a mesh bending 'brake' or clamp which has the advantage of being easy to make, quite small and easy to store when not in use. However for anyone making cages regularly, or in more than small quantities, the 'brake' is quite an unsatisfactory method. What's required in those circumstances is a proper Mesh Bender to give reliable square bends quickly and consistently.

My inspiration for this design came from something I saw during a visit to the factory of the famous A.A.Fenn & Co. Tucked away in a corner was the original mesh bending table that had been used to make the renowned FENN cage traps. What struck me was that here was such a simple tool, which anyone could make and which was clearly very effective indeed.

The model used by FENN was attached to a freestanding table with legs and frame made from angle iron bolted together. The plan detailed below produces just the 'table top', purpose designed to be clamped in a *Black & Decker* style *'Workmate'* or in a bench mounted vice. If you prefer you could always make a dedicated stand but don't forget to include a foot rail to brace against. It's essential that you are able hold the frame steady when you push the wire into shape.

Before you start

Before beginning anything I would recommend that you read the section on *Using the Mesh Bender* towards the end of this chapter. It will be much easier to complete the project, test things as you go and make the necessary choices if you can visualise the final operation.

The most important practical consideration before you begin this project is '*how big are the pieces of mesh that you want to bend?*' It would be incredibly frustrating to build yourself a mesh bending tool only to find it was too small for your next project. Rolls of mesh still seem to come in 3ft widths, although I'm sure they'll catch up with the metric system eventually. I made my own mesh bender an overall width of 1m, to be big enough to take this wire straight off the roll. It makes it a bit on the large side but I know that it will do any job I need it to.

Working from this width – call it '*M*', we need to allow for the width of the washers that will create the gap for the mesh to slide under the bend bar. Allowing 15mm on each end means that the centre of the mounting holes needs to be '*M*' + 30mm apart. Allowing another 25mm on <u>either end</u> from the centre of the holes gives you an overall bend bar length '*L*' which should be '*M*' + 80mm.

These plans are based on an overall Bend Bar length of 1m but these can easily be adjusted for a bender of any width. Overall width 'L' can easily be calculated from the maximum size of mesh you need to work with, '*M*'.

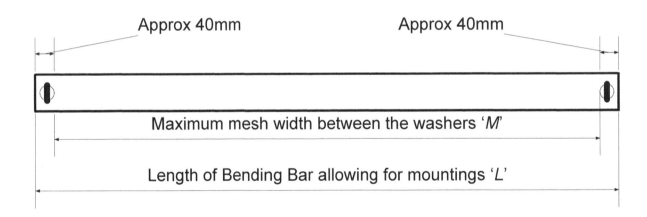

Approx 40mm   Approx 40mm

Maximum mesh width between the washers '*M*'

Length of Bending Bar allowing for mountings '*L*'

Cutting List, Materials & Tools.

Timber

These materials are all standard building sizes available from any builders merchant and most large DIY stores. Exact sizes are not important as long as they all fit together.

- 2 x 1m length (*L*)of 95mm x 40mm planed timber (typically decking joists)
- 1m length (*L*) of 60mm x 35mm planed timber
- 1m length of 20mm dowel
- 3 x Butt hinges – approx 75mm by 40mm, usually brass.
- 2 x M8 Bolts 70mm or 80mm
- 2 x M8 wing nuts
- 2 x M8 square nuts
- M8 penny washers
- 5mm x 70mm screws
- 1m length of Angle iron or flat metal bar

An important choice you need to make before you start is the type of Bending Bar that you're going to use. The longer the bar and the heavier the mesh you'll be bending, the thicker and stronger the bending bar needs to be. The diagrams and photographs in this plan show the use of a flat section bending bar. Angle iron is arguably a better choice, particularly for heavy duty mesh, as the angled section acts as a strengthening rib to prevent bending. The upright part is placed at the back – the mesh is bent on the thin edge not the corner.

Drilling

If you have access to a pillar drill then I recommend that you use it for this project. It is very important that the holes for mounting the Bending bar and fitting the handles are straight and perpendicular to the surface of the wood. You can buy quite inexpensive 'drill stands', which help to hold and steady an ordinary electric drill for projects like this.

If you must use a hand drill, take your time and have a practice first on some scrap wood. Use a small spirit level to help position the drill correctly, but when drilling keep the work area clear.

Other Tools

- Hand Clamp
- Saw
- Drill with 2mm, 4.5mm, 7.5mm and 20mm bits
- Screwdriver
- Bradawl

Exploded Schematic Diagram

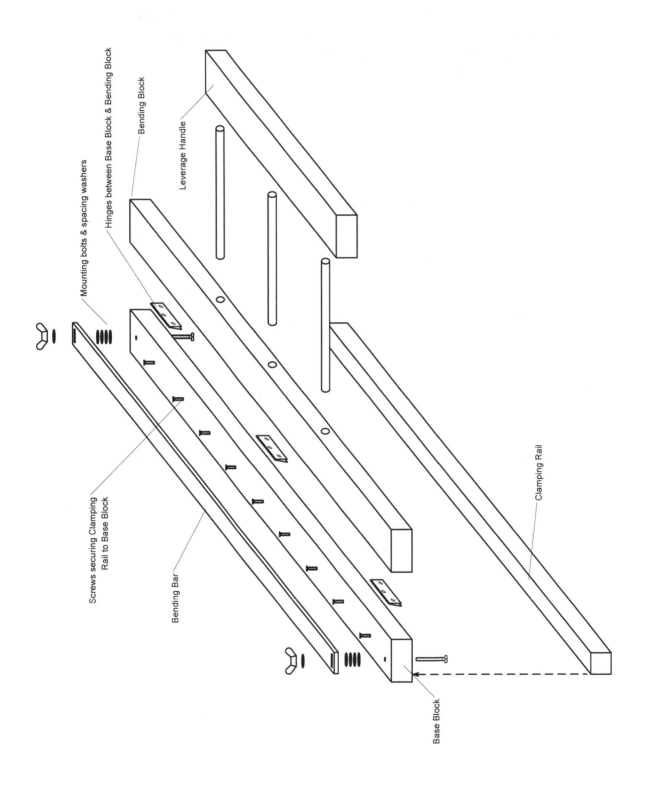

Mounting bolts & spacing washers

Hinges between Base Block & Bending Block

Bending Block

Leverage Handle

Screws securing Clamping Rail to Base Block

Bending Bar

Clamping Rail

Base Block

Assembly instructions

Preparing the Bending Bar

See **Options & Variations** for the differences when using angle iron for the Bending Bar.

1   Take the metal bending bar and place it on the bench. Mark a line down the centre of one flat side.

2   From each end, measure in 20mm and mark a line at right angles to the line drawn in step 1. This will give you a cross at each end identifying where the mounting holes need to go.

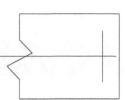

3   Drill an 8mm mounting hole at each point centred on the cross marked. Ideally the mounting hole should be oval (8 mm by 30mm) as that allows you to adjust the position of the bending bar for different mesh thicknesses and to 'tune' the bender after final assembly.   It's best if you can get this done by someone with access to a milling machine, but it can be done by drilling several holes close together along the line (see Options & Variation). Worst case a single mounting hole on the marked cross will do the job.

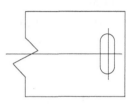

Preparing the Base Block

4   Take one length of 95mm x 40mm timber and place it on the bench to begin creating the Base Block.

5   Place the Bending Bar on the Bending Block; level along one of the long edges and central end to end.

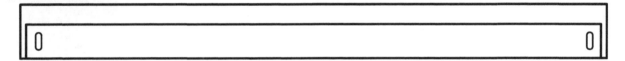

If you are using a single mount hole, rather than a slot, position the bar approximately 5mm back from the long parallel edge.

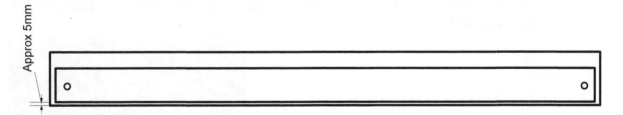

6 Mark through the mounting holes of the Bar onto the Block.

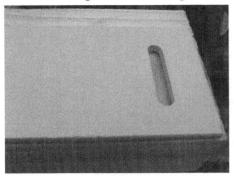 

7 Lift off the bar and write 'Underside' on the face of the Base Block that you've just marked.

8 Mark the midpoint of each of the Mounting Hole ovals you've drawn. Use a marking gague to ensure that each mark is the same distance, from the same edge, at both ends.

9 Take a large drill bit the same diameter as the bolt head, (usually 20mm), and clamp the base Block so that you can work at one end. Where you have marked in Step 7, drill a very shallow hole about 4mm deep. This is to accomodate the head of the bolt so that it doesn't stick out above the surface of the Block.

10 Test that this hole is deep enough by using the bolt head upside down.

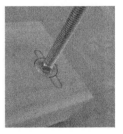

11 Next take a 7.5mm drill and position it in the centre of the shallow hole. Most wide drill bits have a central spike which will have left a pefect starter hole. Drill right through the block to the other side. (The hole is 7.5mm so that it's slightly smaller than bolt and will ensure a tight fit.)

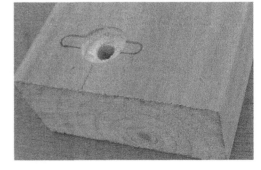

12 Repeat steps 7 to 11 at the other end.

13 Turn the Base Block over and write 'Top' on the upward surface.

14 Now mark a line down the centre of this Top face.
    Starting from one end mark on this line roughly every 50 mm. This is where the screws
    will go which secure the Base Block to the Clamping rail. Adjust the spacing as
    necessary to ensure that these holes do not interfere with the holes already drilled for the
    bolts.

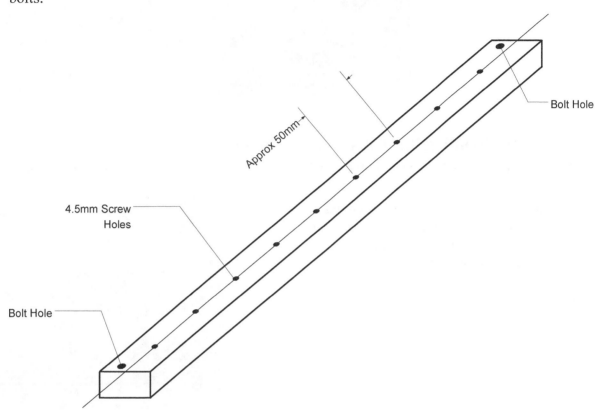

15 Using a 4.5mm drill bit, drill though at each of these marks. Countersink the holes on the
    Top face only.

16 The Base Block should now look like this.

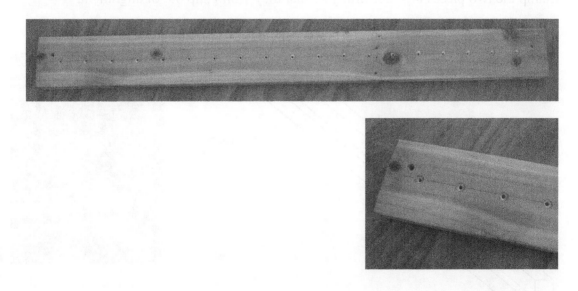

17 Turn the Base Block over and clean up the reverse of the drilled holes to remove any broken fibres or debris. This is important to make sure that the Base Block and the Clamping Rail fit together tightly.

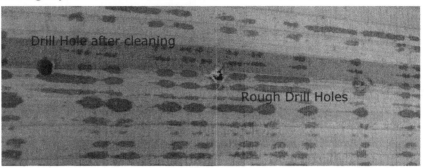

Fitting the Bending Bar bolts and Clamping Rail

18 Place the Base Block back on the bench making sure that the 'Underside' is upwards.

19 Push the two bolts into the mounting holes at either end. Use a hammer to gently tap them all the way through. The head of the bolt should fit into the shallow recess you created in step 9.

20 Place the Clamping Rail onto the Base Block approximately along the centre line. Measure carefully from one edge of the Base Block to the edge of the Clamping Rail to ensure that they are parallel.

   Clamp the two pieces together firmly so that they won't slip out of alignment.

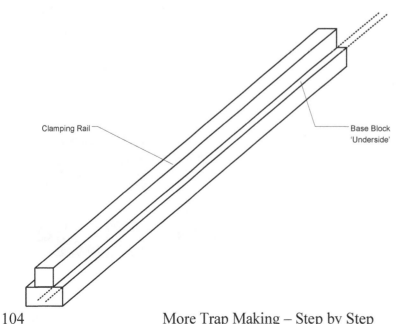

21 Turn the Base Block over so that the Clamping rail is underneath and the 'Top' side is uppermost.

22 Insert and tighten screws through each of the holes along the centre line to fix the Base Block and the Clamping Rail together.

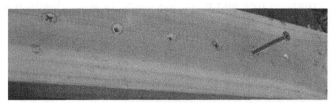

Remove the clamps.

23 Place 3 or 4 spacer washers onto each mounting bolt. Alternatively place on one washer and then fit and tighten a single square nut and place a washer on top.

24 Check that the Bending Bar fits correctly onto the mounting bolts. Align it about 5mm back from the edge of the Base Block and secure with a washer and wing nut on each bolt.

25 Take one of the hinges and position it on the edge of the Base Block at one end and on the edge closest to where you've just fitted the Bending Bar. The barrel of the hinge should be closest to the Top of the Base Block. The hinge should be stepped down about 5mm from the Top of the Base Block (see photo in step 28).

26 Mark through the screw holes in the hinge onto the Base Block and mark the bottom edge of the hinge.

27 Remove the hinge and using a marking gauge continue this line along the full length of the Base Block. Position a second hinge at the other end taking care to line it up on the marked line and mark the screw holes. Position and mark the third hinge in the centre, again on the marked line.

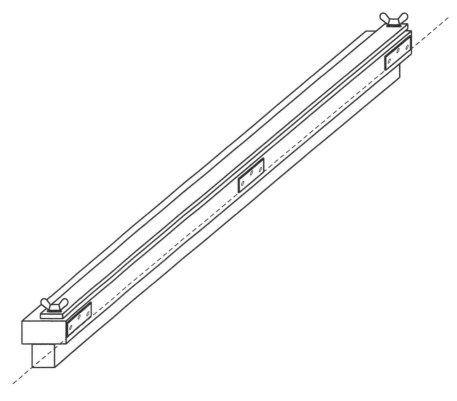

28 Using a 2mm drill bit pre-drill pilot holes for each of the screws.

Carefully reposition the hinges one at a time and screw them into place. Take extra care to ensure that they remain aligned to the guide line.

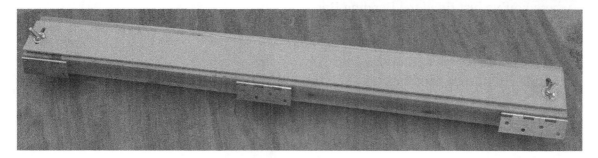

Assembling the Bending Block & Handle

How you make and attach the handle for the bending block is really up to you and the method shown here is only one approach. Essentially you just need to create a lever which will enable you to apply firm and even pressure to the Bending Block when you're bending the mesh. In these instructions I have used a long 'handle' with three strong dowel rods connecting it to the Bending Block. On a small bender you might get away with using two but I would advise against having only one as it will have quite a lot of force applied to it.

Of course you don't have to use this approach at all; you'll notice in the photograph of the FENN original that a simple plank of wood has been used, screwed to the bottom of the Bending Block.

One other thing to remember is that the longer the handles are the easier it will be to bend the mesh, but make them too long and they'll get in the way and be impractical.

29 Take the Leverage Handle and stand it up on edge. Using a marking gauge, mark a line down the centre. Then use a rule and carpenters square to mark the midpoint length ways and the quarter points

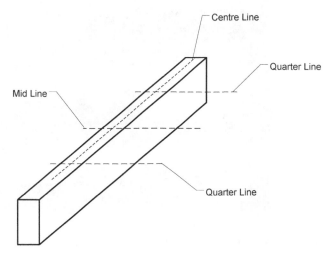

30 Now take the bending bar and mark the centre line and midpoint line in the same way. Place the two blocks side by side and line up the mid lines. Use a carpenters square to transfer across the quarter lines marked on the Handle.

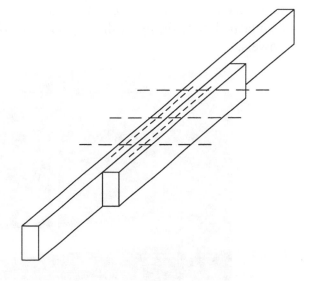

31 Mark where the lines cross. Drill holes, the thickness of the dowell, at these cross points. Make sure the holes are perpendicular to the surface and use a pillar drill if you have one. These holes should be deep but not go all way through.

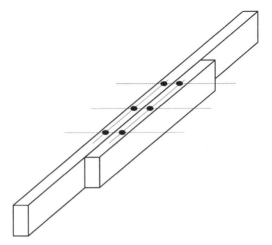

32 Laid out as in the photograph below, apply glue to the holes and using a wooden mallet gently tap the dowels into the handle

33 Lift and turn the handle so that the dowels are downwards and fit them to the holes on the bending bar. Tap home with a mallet and check that everything is fitted in square.

34 Leave the glue to dry before moving onto the final assembly. If necessary the dowels can be attached more firmly by drilling and screwing through the Block into the the side of the dowels.

Fitting the Bending Block

35 The final assembly is quite simple, but can be a bit awkward, particularly if you've made a large and heavy version. An extra pair of hands might come in handy.
Begin by putting the assembled Base Block onto the bench UPSIDE DOWN with the hinge towards you.

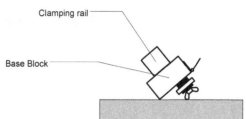

36 Open the hinge a little so that you can get in behind it as you'll need to mark the screw holes.

37 Take the Bending Block and bring it up against the hinges. Align the edge of the Bending Block so that it's in position against the hinge and then mark through one hole of a hinge at each end. It's not impossible to do on your own, but this is where the extra pair of hands really helps.

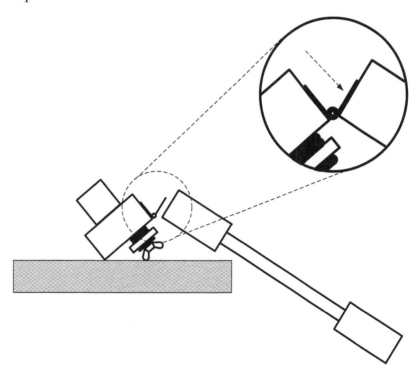

38 Take the Bending Block away again and using a bradawl or large nail, make starter holes at the points you have marked. Insert and tighten screws at just these two points.

39 Carefully turn the hole thing over and check to see that when you push them together, the Bending Block closes parrallel against the Bending Bar. Remember you only have a couple of screws in place at this stage - don't use too much force or you'll pull them out.

40 If they are not parrallel take the time to work out which end you need to adjust and by how much. It can help to mark the hinge you need to change. Once you're satisfied you know what's needed, turn it back over again and remove the screw from the misaligned hinge.

41 Reposition the Bending Block and mark a new screw position *through a different hole in the hinge*. If you use the same place on the hinge it will be hard to avoid the hole you made the first time.

42 Repeat Steps 38-40 until you're happy with the alignment.

43 When everything lines up correctly, turn the assembly back over; mark and start all the holes for the hinges and fix all the screws.

Your Mesh bender is now complete !

Using the Mesh Bender

Basic Operation

To use the Mesh bender you first need to fix it firmly, into a bench mounted vice or a B*lack and Decker* style *workmate*. Do this with the Bending Block in the flat position and check that you have the full range of movement up and down.

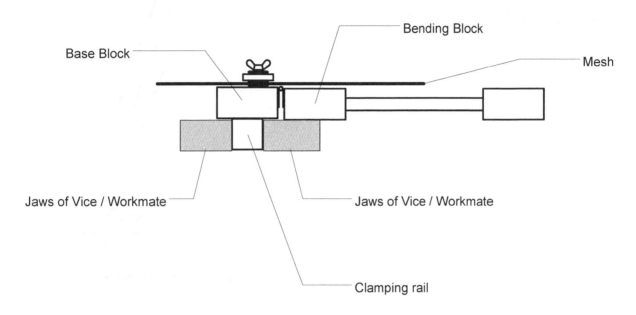

To bend a piece of mesh, insert it flat across the top of the Base and Bending blocks and under the Bending Bar. Use the grid of the mesh itself to align it straight along the edge of the Bending Bar.

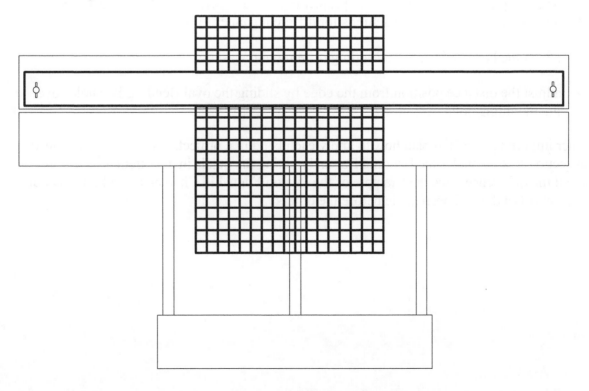

Raise the handle a little until it begins to push on the mesh sheet. This tension will now keep the mesh in place and allow you to let go of the mesh.

Continue to raise the handle on the Bending Block in a smooth action, bending the mesh against the edge of the Bending Bar.

On heavier mesh you will usually need to brace the Workmate so that it does not tip up – just put your foot on the step that's provided.

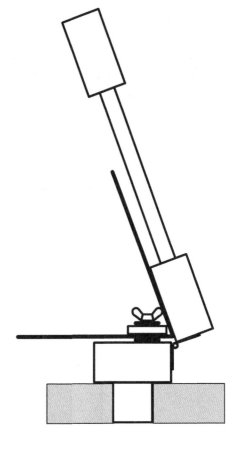

Things to consider.

Before beginning a serious mesh bending project it pays to experiment a bit and get used to what works best. Try out different settings for different gauges of mesh:

- adjust the height of the bar by adding or removing washers.

- adjust the distance position from the edge by sliding the oval Bending Bar holes over the mounting bolts.

Another important step is to plan how to apply each bend in a project. You will always need a flat section to slide under the Bending Bar and making the bends in a particular order can make all the difference. See the example of the Pigeon Funnel in Chapter 12 and think about the impact if Bend 3 had been made before the others.

Design Options & Variations

Making an oval slot using the multiple hole technique:

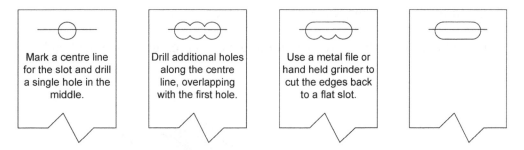

Mark a centre line for the slot and drill a single hole in the middle.	Drill additional holes along the centre line, overlapping with the first hole.	Use a metal file or hand held grinder to cut the edges back to a flat slot.	

Use of Angle Iron for the Bending Bar

Angle iron makes an excellent Bending Bar as the perpendicular section forms a strengething 'rib' which stops the bar from bending upwards when under pressue from the mesh.

The important thing to remember is that the upright section goes at the rear – the mesh needs to be bent agains a flat edge and not a corner.

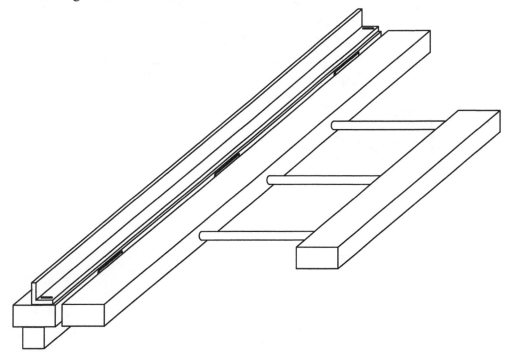

Alternative handle

An alternative to the handle given in the plan is to simply screw a long section of plywood to the bottom of the Bending Block. Remember to put a piece of the same material on the Base Block as well before you fit the Clamping Rail so that the undersides are level.

Avoid a single small handle as it will be more difficult to get even pressure along the bend.

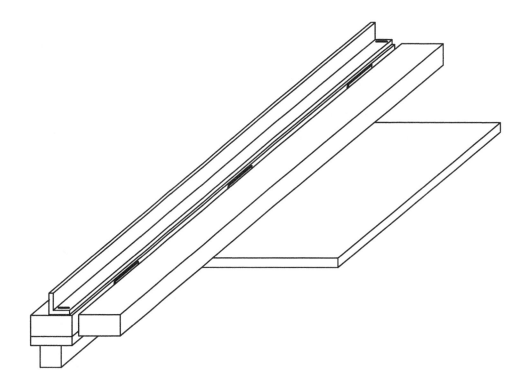

Chapter 8 - The Mouse Funnel Trap

This traditional trap is another great example of the 'passive door' at work. In Trap Making Step by Step I explained how funnels could be used very effectively in traps for birds. This design uses the same principle in a multi-catch trap for mice with no moving parts and no trigger. Commercial traps based on this idea have been available for a long time and you can still buy them today if you look hard enough.

The particular plan given here is also a great example of how designs can evolve and improve through discussion and the sharing of ideas. The basics of the trap were first shown to me by a friend living in France - his initial pictures showing just how effective it could be. After I built a prototype for this book, I managed to film the trap in action and you can see some of that footage on the Fourteenacre website. Inspired by my posts on one of the internet hunting forums, 'Carnie' built his own version and came up with the brilliantly simple idea for the access door.

This plan was tested for me by two students at Aith Junior High School on Shetland. I had been in dialogue with the Craft and Design Department for several months and together we thought it might make an interesting project. Not only did the boys make the excellent version of the trap pictured here, they also came up with an improvement to the design.

The boys found that the wire rod, which locks the door shut, was difficult to keep in place when moving the trap about, for example when going to release the mice elsewhere. After trying a few ideas the boys devised a shepherd's crook shape similar to an extended R-pin. With this design the locking pin is held in place during use but is easy to remove. The one shown in this picture they made themselves and it works well.

The mesh used in this plan is quite lightweight but with relatively small holes – about 7mm square available in sheets in most garden centres. It is also regularly used to make the popular wire mesh peanut feeders for birds. I have seen these traps made with 10mm square mesh which may do, but I certainly wouldn't go any larger; mice can fit through surprisingly small gaps.

I always recommend that you read each plan through before you get started, but in this case it is especially true. Apart from a few key dimensions, (cage height, funnel diameter and the gap between funnel and floor), you can make this trap in any shape and size you want.

Cutting List & Materials

- 12mm exterior grade plywood sizes as shown
- Sections of wire mesh sizes as shown. Mesh size approx 7mm but no larger than 10mm
  Note: always cut to complete squares of mesh. If measurements fall in the middle of a square always cut larger, not smaller. It can always be trimmed later if necessary.
- A 1mm or 2mm thick wire rod length 160mm
- 30mm wire nails
- 4 'U' shaped wire staples (Screw-eyes are optional to replace 2 of the 'U' staples).
- More wire staples or staple gun for fixing mesh
- Cage clips, cable ties or short lengths of wire

Tools

- Saw
- Hammer
- Drill with 3.5 mm & 4mm bit
- Screwdriver
- Bradawl
- Wire Cutters

Useful if you have them:

- Staple gun
- Cage clip pliers

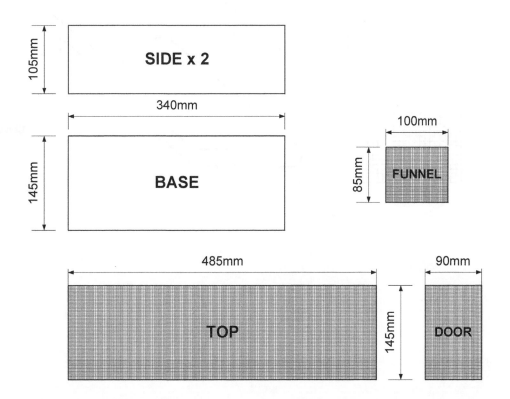

Exploded Schematic Diagram

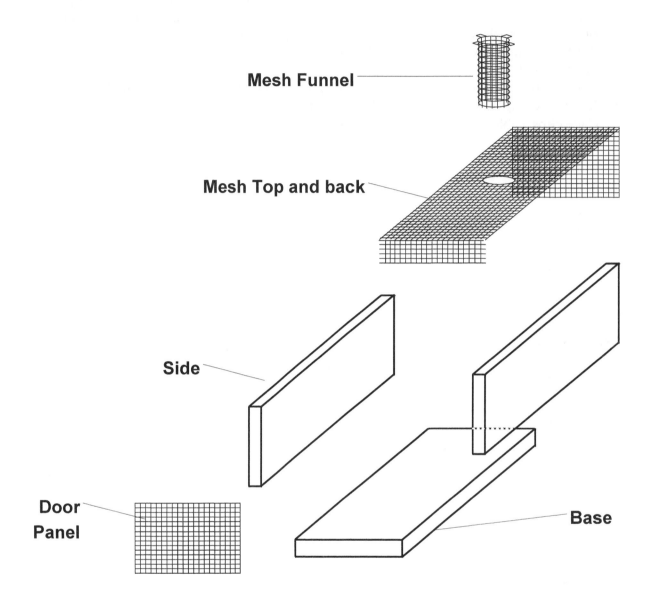

Mesh Funnel

Mesh Top and back

Side

Door Panel

Base

More Trap Making – Step by Step

Assembly instructions

Making the Box

1   Take the base board and mark a line about 5mm in from each of the long edges. Take 6 to 8 nails, (half along each side), and at roughly equal intervals start the nails off along the marked lines.

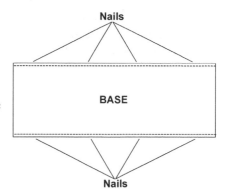

2   Stand the two sides edge down on the bench and about the right distance apart. Place the base board on top, nails up. Carefully line up one side with the base and hammer in the nails for that side. Then repeat for the other side. Turn it over and you will have the basic box shape

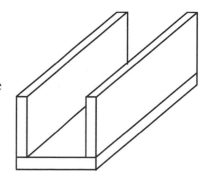

Fitting the Trap Top

3   Take the wooden box frame and stand it on one end.

4   Take the largest piece of the mesh and lay it over the upwards end of the wooden box frame. Make sure that the mesh is flush with the outer edge of the base and both sides.

Using the staple gun or wire staples secure the mesh to the edge of the base and sides.

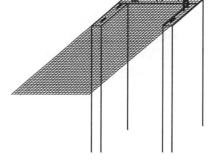

5   Carefully bend the mesh down to cover the top of the trap and rotate the whole box so that it rests on the bench the right way up.

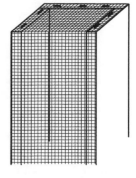

6   Keeping the mesh tight and making sure that it is
     flush with the outer edges of both sides, use the
     staple gun or wire staples secure the mesh to the
     wooden sides of the box.

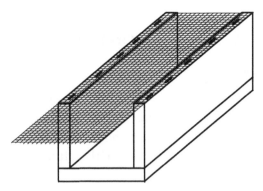

7   Carefully bend the mesh down to cover the remaining
     end of the trap. **NOTE** it should only reach about a
     quarter to a third of the way down. Trim if necessary.

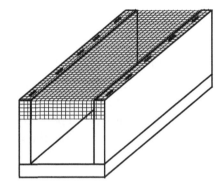

8   Rotate the whole box so that it rests on the end that is already covered
     with mesh. Secure the remaining mesh with staple gun or wire staples
     but AVOID PLACING ANY STAPLES IN THE LAST HOLE OF
     THE MESH.

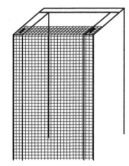

Fitting the Release Door

9   Take the piece of mesh for the door and place it on the end of the box so that it meets the edge of the main roof piece. Trim the door so that it fits the height of the box. If the squares of the mesh align awkwardly with the bottom edge of the box, then leave the mesh a little over long for now.

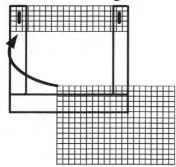
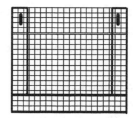

10 Now remove a few strands of the mesh to create two holes that line up with the bottom of the wooden frame. These need to be big enough for your staples or screw-eyes to pass through edge on.

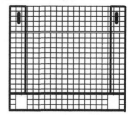

11 Reposition the door on the end of the trap box and carefully hammer in a pair of wire staples across the gap where the two pieces of mesh join. DO NOT hammer these in fully as they form the hinge for the door to open. Place the trap the right way up on the bench and check that the door opens and closes.

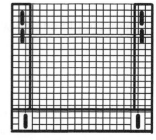

12 Next insert the last two staples (or screw-eyes if preferred) into the end of the wooden frames so that that pass through the holes made in step 10. These will form the locking rings.

13 Take the length of wire rod and make a bend about 20mm from one end. Using this as a handle, slide the rod through the locking rings to hold the door closed. Check that the door is held tightly against the frame and that there are no gaps a mouse could push through. If necessary remove the rod and push the locking rings into the frame a little further.

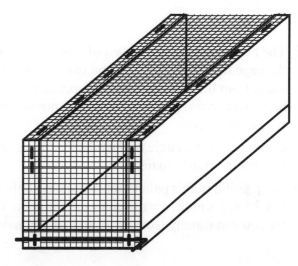

Making the Funnel

14 Take the small rectangle of mesh and prepare to roll the **long length** up into a tube 80mm long.

15 In order to get a good even tube shape you need to bend the mesh square around something, known as a 'former'. Anything will do as long as it's about 25mm diameter; a broom handle is usually ideal. Small plastic water pipes or small deodorant aerosols may also be suitable.

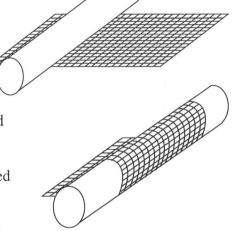

Don't be tempted to just roll it by hand – use whatever you can find that closest to the right size and then just gently pull the tube to the correct diameter. If you're using 7mm mesh then the sides of the tube should overlap by 2 rows. The diameter of the finished tube should be approximately 25mm.

16 Using the cage clips, cable ties or wire twists secure the overlapping section in 3 places. You may need to enlarge the mesh holes to fit the cable ties or clips. Fasten the tube as close to one end as possible, roughly in the middle of the tube and at least 10mm in from the other end – from now on the 'top' of the funnel.

The distance from the top of the highest joint to the bottom of the funnel shouldn't be more than 70mm or the funnel will be too long.

You should end up with neat, straight and firm tube of wire.

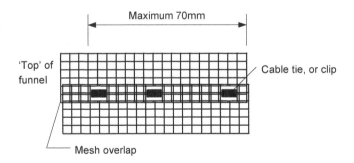

17 The next step is to make a set of tabs at the top of the tube to help secure it to the mesh of the cage top. Take the tube and using your wire cutters carefully remove one square of mesh from the top 1 or 2 rows, depending on what size mesh you're using. (In effect just removing some of the wire crosspieces).

18 Count round the circle of the tube 2 squares and then remove the third square.

19 Keep going in this pattern until you get all the way round. You will probably find that you have a single row of squares at the end. This doesn't matter but if you plan ahead a bit you can usually work it out so that you have two 'three' blocks instead.

20 Now gently bend each of the pairs of squares downwards and outwards until they are sticking out at right angles to the sides of the tube. When you come to fit the tube to the trap top these tabs will prevent the tube from dropping straight through the hole and will perform as fixing tags.

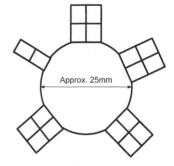

This diagram shows the view looking down the funnel from the top end.

Fitting the Funnel

21 Take the completed trap box and place it right way up on the bench. Use the diagonals from the trap corners to identify and mark the approximate centre of the trap mesh top.

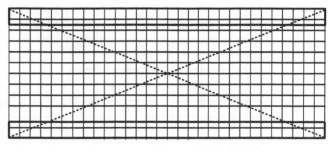

22 Place your funnel on this centre spot and using a felt pen or marker draw around it, leaving a the circle indicated on the mesh. Obviously the holes on the mesh means that you won't get a complete circle but the marks on the wires will be enough. This will become the hole that the funnel fits into.

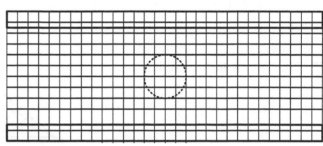

23 Carefully cutaway a square that just fits the outside of the circle. If you have to go a little bigger than the diagram shows don't worry as the tabs on the funnel will help to cover any gaps.
If you do have a disaster and cut a hole which is too big, simply make a collar of mesh to sit over the hole.
(See Options & Variations: Funnel Mount Repair Collar)

24 Insert the bottom of the funnel through the hole you have just made and gently push it through until the tabs rest on the surface of the mesh.

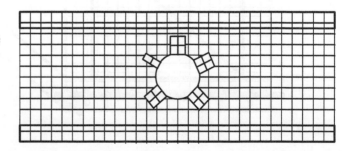

25 Check that the bottom of the funnel is approximately 30mm away from the base of the trap box. If this gap is too large the mice will be able to escape.

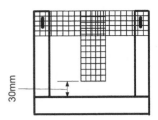

26 Using cable ties, cage clips, lock wire or simple wire twists secure the tags to the mesh of the trap top.

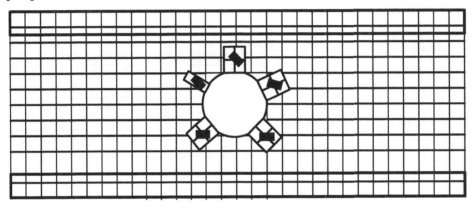

27 The Trap is now complete.

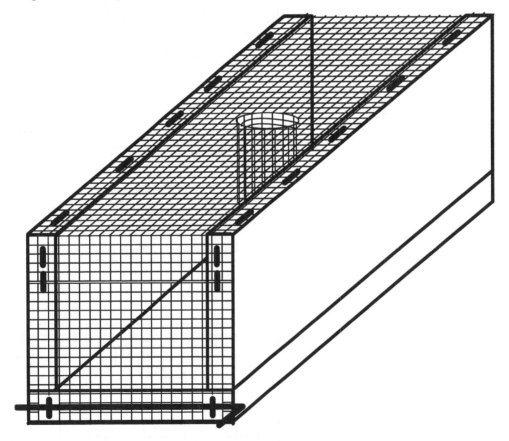

Using the Trap

The Fourteenacre website includes a night camera video of this type of trap in action. It is fascinating to watch the mouse trying to find his way into the trap and be completely unable to find the way back out.

The trap should be generously baited and placed on a surface where the mice are known to be active. My preferred bait for this trap is a couple of handfuls of wild bird food scattered across the bottom of the trap box. Loose bait like this does tend to move about and can tip out when you're removing the captured mice.

Check the trap twice daily, particularly first thing in the morning. There is nothing humane about leaving a mouse to die of thirst in a live catch trap.

When you find that the trap has caught, the mice will also be aware of you and very frightened. Cover the entire trap with an old tea towel or similar to minimise any distress if you are moving the mice to be released elsewhere. To release the mice carefully set the trap down on the floor and roll the tea towel back from the door end. Slide out the locking rod, prop open the door and take a few steps back. If the mice do not leave after a few minutes carefully remove the tea towel completely and stand behind the closed end.

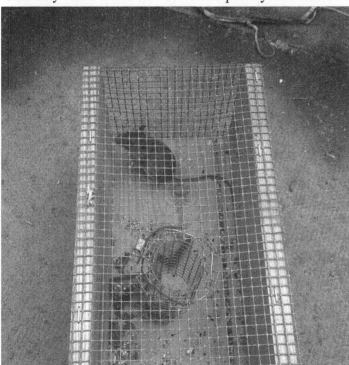

If the trap fails to catch it will be for one of three reasons:

The mice are no longer active in that area: Leave some bait outside the trap and see if that is taken, or sprinkle a little flour around the trap and look for any signs of activity.

The mice are not entering the trap: Look for signs that the bait inside the trap has been disturbed to confirm whether mice are getting in. Check that there is enough room for them to exit the bottom of the funnel and place some bait on top of the trap near the entry funnel. It is always possible that the mice cannot enter the funnel as they are in fact rats and too big!

The mice are escaping: Most likely this will because the funnel exit is too high or the funnel itself is too wide. Try pinching the ends of the tube together slightly into an oval shape or inserting an inner funnel as described in Options & Variations.

Options & Variations

General

There is no particular reason for the trap box to be rectangular. The outer shape could just as easily be square, circular, triangular or any other shape. Avoid anything too narrow though as you do not want the funnel to be too close to the sides.

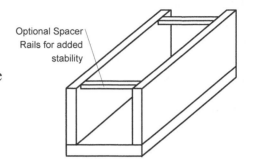

Optional Spacer Rails for added stability

If the structure of the wooden box seems too weak, a pair of simple spacing rails can be added between the walls near each end. This can be made of roofing lath, dowel or anything similar and held in place by a couple of nails.

If you opt for a large trap then multiple funnels should be used – you want to make it fairly easy for the mice to find the way in.

Keep at least one wall of the trap as mesh, two is preferable. Mesh sides make it easier for mice outside the trap to see and smell the bait, and later on to see and smell the mice already caught. I also believe that it makes it easier for the mice to climb up onto the top of the trap which is where we want them.

The Funnel

The diameter of the funnel and the distance from the bottom of the funnel to the trap floor are the only really significant things you need to stick to.

The funnel given in this plan is the typical diameter used for this type of trap. The widest diameter that I have used is 35mm, formed around a rotary washing line pole and the narrowest I have seen was 23mm in diameter. It is quite simple to make a set of 2 or 3 funnels which can be used to adjust the trap when in operation – make and fit a 35mm tube first and the smaller funnels can simply be pushed down inside the fitted one to reduce the internal size of the tube.

The gap between the opening at the base of funnel and the floor of the trap should be 30mm. A few millimetres difference either way won't matter too much, but too low and the mice won't get through, too high and they'll find the way out.

Some designs I have seen also leave the upright strands of mesh long to create 'fingers' at the end of the tunnel just to close the entrance up a little bit more.

Alternative Release Doors

There are a couple of alternative options for the release door that can be borrowed straight from the plan for the See-Saw traps given in Trap Making Step by Step.

A routed groove at one end of the box would enable the use of a vertical sliding door – made either from a piece of thicker mesh or wooden frame and mesh

A simple frame and mesh door could also be hinges of the box framework, with a locking toggle.

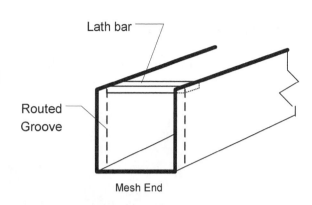

Lath bar

Routed Groove

Mesh End

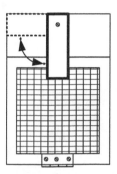

The Funnel Mount Repair Collar

If you should accidentally cut the hole for the funnel too big, or at a later date want to swap the funnel for a smaller one, there is no need to replace the trap mesh covering. Simply cut a mesh collar, larger than the hole in the trap mesh and with the correct sized hole in its centre. Then just insert the collar between the trap and funnel when you fit the funnel.

Step 1

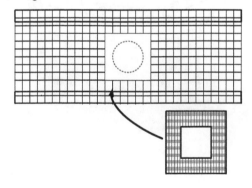

Step 2

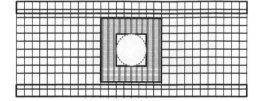

Step 3

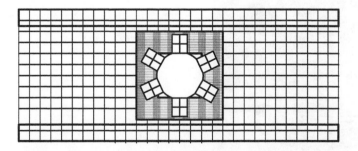

Historic & Commercial Examples

These are a few examples of commercially produced traps that use the same principle. I hope that they will further inspire you do develop your own versions of the trap.

Round mesh

Chapter 9 – The Fly Trap

This is another example of the efficient and highly effective 'funnel' at work. Just as with the mouse trap there are just a few key dimensions and principles that make this trap design work. In this trap however, you'll notice that the funnel is used upside down.

I decided to include this design following some research into American traps and in particular a trap manufactured by Olsen & Thompson in the 1930s. The one pictured is the later, slightly smaller, mass produced model which stands 8.5 inches high and roughly 4.25 inches in diameter.

There is a photograph of an earlier model on the Fourteenacre website. That one is a much larger 11 ¼ inches high and 6 ½ inches diameter so there may have been several sizes in manufacture through its development.

Broadly speaking, you can make the shape and size of the outer catch chamber whatever you want provided that you get the funnel right. These ones are cylindrical but you can make them square or even triangular if you want to.

This picture shows William Simunek of Cleveland Ohio, USA with a trap he built himself in August 1952. His large scale trap was inspired by ones like those manufactured by Olsen & Thompson. He'd remembered those being sold but as they were no longer widely available he just made his own.

The basics of the design in both these cases differ significantly from the 'hanging' traps that are still sold today, usually for wasps. Those traps rely on bait inside to draw the insects in, where as this design captures the flies as they leave the bait.

For some projects in this book the measurements and materials are critical for a successful working outcome. However as there is so much flexibility with this trap it is an excellent opportunity for a bit of experimentation and design initiative.

Why make a fly Trap?

Fly traps of this type fell out of favour during the second half of the 20th Century, as chemical sprays became cheap, easy to use and virtually instant. Although certainly more controlled now than they used to be, these sprays may not always be safe for use in confined areas or around particular types of pets and fish. They can also kill other beneficial insects, can damage the environment and become expensive to use long term. Domestic sprays are of limited use in the open air and can run out just when you need them most.

A well built fly trap can be baited with a huge range of substances, is extremely long lasting, has no moving parts to wear out and used as a permanent technique will control flies very effectively. One of these sat on top of your ferret cage or dog run could help significantly to keep fly numbers in check. With the basic principle understood you can see how easy it is to make similar traps in all sorts of shapes and sizes, from all sorts of materials.

Key features, principles & measurements

- **Catch Chamber**
  The catch chamber should ideally be made from thin, fine mesh, with holes small enough that the flies cannot escape. All the traps of this style that I have seen use a mesh of some sort or sometimes a transparent solid material such as plastic or historically glass. A critical element of these traps is that light above the funnel encourages the flies to go upwards into the catch chamber.

- **Funnel**
  The inverted funnel is the other critical element of the trap. It should extend to about half the height of the trap inside the catch chamber and the small opening at the tip should be about 8 -10 mm in diameter. In all the traps of this design that I have seen, the funnel height is about the same as its diameter.

  The lower end, the large opening, should cover a big proportion of the bottom of the catch chamber. The rest of the base of the catch chamber should be solid, so that light is only visible through the funnel, attracting the flies upwards.

  Soft mesh or netting is an unsuitable material for the funnel as it needs to be self supporting. If you have to use netting then make a framework funnel from larger holed wire mesh and then cover it with your fine net.

- **Access for Emptying**
  The ring at the top of the catch chamber should be fitted with an access lid of some type – usually a disc of wood or metal pivoted on a nail. This is essential in order to empty the dead flies from the trap.

- **Supports**

  However you decide to make the trap, it must include short legs to hold the base of the trap above the standing surface. Typically the wide opening of the funnel should be about 25mm above the standing surface.

- **Skirt**

  The creation of a semi enclosed area below the funnel makes it more difficult for flies to fly out sideways. On the round traps this is achieved through a 'skirt' of mesh reducing access to a narrow crawl strip about 10mm high. In the square trap shown at the start of this chapter the same effect is achieved by placing the bait raised within the mouth of the funnel.

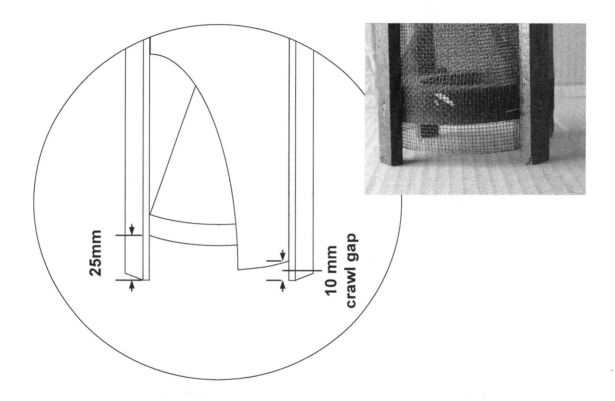

Making a copy of the Olsen & Thompson Trap.

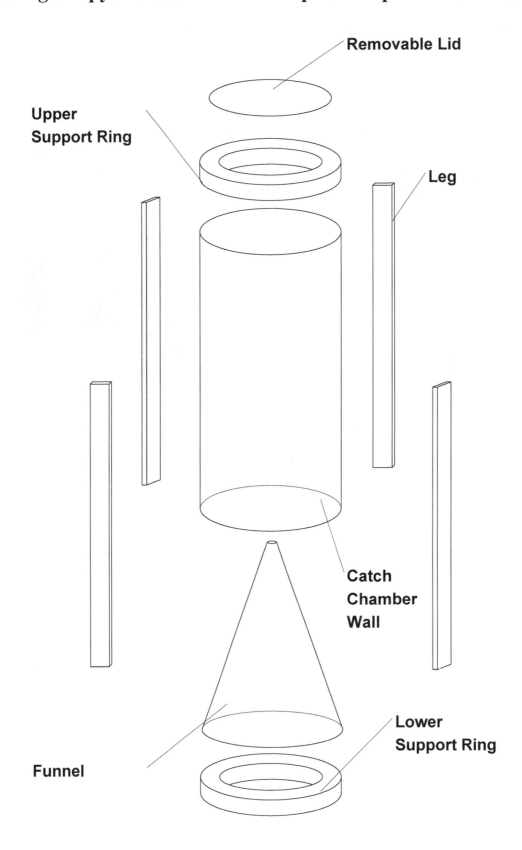

Removable Lid

Upper
Support Ring

Leg

Catch
Chamber
Wall

Lower
Support Ring

Funnel

Main Components

Support Rings

The support rings are usually made of wood – solid softwood, medium density fibreboard (MDF) or even plywood. If you have access to a lathe, or to a friend with a lathe, then that is by far the easiest and quickest way to create the rings. They don't need to be terribly strong or deep as there is no real weight in the trap. However they do need to be thick enough for you to nail or screw the trap legs onto.

There is no reason why plastic or metal couldn't be used for the rings but you need to think ahead and work out how all the fixings would be achieved.

Another alternative is to use rings of strong, thick wire; the mesh could be 'sewn' into place around the wire ring and the legs lock-wired in position.

For the funnel in the project photos I have used MDF rings with an outside diameter 110mm and an inside of 65mm.

Mesh

Commercial metal fly mesh is really the ideal material to use if you can obtain any - and if you can only get a little save it for the funnel.   Nylon fly mesh 'netting' is easily available from most DIY stores in black or white and usually as part of a pack with a self-adhesive frame to fix around door and windows in the summer.

Where the metal mesh scores above the netting is that it is rigid enough to be self supporting. This helps with the overall stability of a trap like the Olsen & Thompson but it is crucial for the funnel.

If you can _only_ get the netting then you will need to make a framework for the funnel shape, using some 19 gauge mesh or similar. Then you can fix the netting over that framework.

Upright legs

These are the least specific part of the trap. Anything will do, as long as they can be attached to the Support Rings and are strong enough to support the weight and shape of the trap. In the photographs in this chapter I have used 25mm x 6mm softwood strip, sold in the moulding section of most major DIY stores and builders merchants.

Assembly Instructions

1. Make the funnel.

Before you begin doing anything with your mesh, particularly if you don't have very much, I strongly suggest that you practice making a funnel using a piece of stiff paper or thin card. Go through all of these steps and once you're quite happy that your cone will turn out as required mark and cut a final template. Place it under the mesh and hold it in place with a clip or even a couple of staples. Then cut the mesh round the template.

Use a half circle with radius equal to approx 1.5 times the height you want you cone to be. For the funnel in project photos I wanted a 100mm funnel so have used a radius of 150mm.

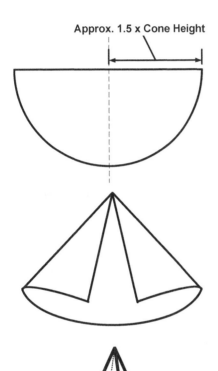

Approx. 1.5 x Cone Height

Taking the two outside corners of the flat edge, curl them round and bring them together to form a cone.

Overlap the edges until the base of the cone forms a circle just a little larger than the <u>outside</u> of the BOTTOM support ring. The ring needs to be able to fit inside the base of the cone.

Use an ordinary household stapler to temporarily fix the overlapping sections together. Check that the support ring fits.

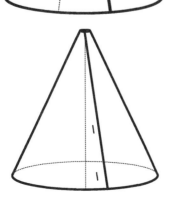

Test that the hole at the top of the funnel is about the right size – you should just be able to slide a pencil through it.

Fix the cone shape using a stapler or a needle and a length of fine wire or strong thread, sew through the mesh to secure the join.

2. Fix the Funnel to the ring.

Place the base of the funnel over one of the rings and position it so that the cone is upright and more or less central.

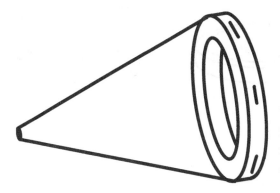

Use a stapler or small tacks to fix the cone in place in three or four places. It will be fixed more firmly in place as you assemble the rest of the trap.

Test again that the hole at the top of the funnel is still about the right size and if necessary adjust the cone. The mesh is quite pliable and with care can be adjusted.

3. **Fix lid to top ring**

Place the trap lid onto the top ring and mark a place to drill a hole that will correspond to the middle of the thickness of the ring.

Drill a hole and fix the lid to the ring with a short screw, not too tight though, so that the lid can pivot open and closed.

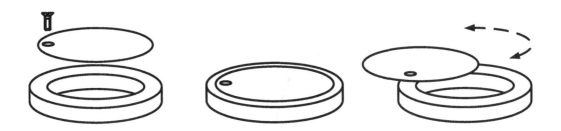

On one ring measure and mark lines at the four quarter points on the circle. Line up the second ring and carry these marks over. Make sure they match up on both rings.

4. Measure the height of the upright legs (for this project they were 215mm long). Deduct 10 mm for the crawl gap and this gives you 'H', the height of the mesh panel.

5. On each leg mark two lines – one where the mesh should align to and one where the bottom of the ring will sit. In our project 10mm and 25mm respectively.

6. Measure round the outside circumference of the rings and add 2cm or more for overlap. This gives you 'W', the width of the mesh panel. (On this project, that worked out to be 360mm)

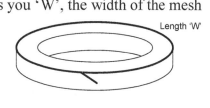

Length 'W'

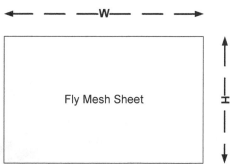

Height 'H'

10 mm crawl gap

7. Measure and cut a section of mesh W by H or 360mm by 205mm if you're following the project in the photographs.

W

Fly Mesh Sheet

H

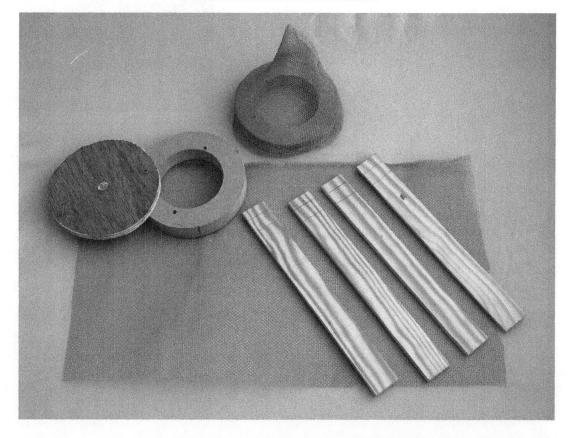

8. Take the two rings and fix one of the legs in place across both. This is to help hold the rings in place while you add the mesh and is only temporary - so don't screw it on too tight.

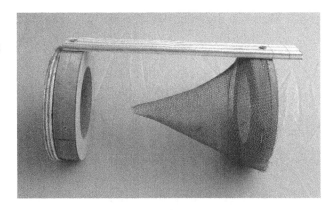

Make sure the leg is lined up with a 'quarter mark' on each ring and with the height mark on the leg itself.

9. Place the mesh onto the rings, allowing enough to overlap past the attached leg.

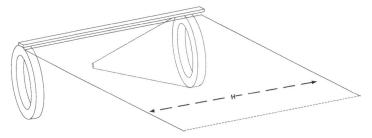

Line the mesh up with care to the marks on the first leg and the second leg as you fix that in place.

Staple the mesh to the rings as you go.

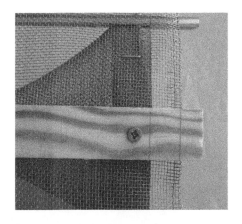

I had cut the mesh a little too wide and you can see in this photograph that it is overlapping the top ring. This can easily be trimmed off later.

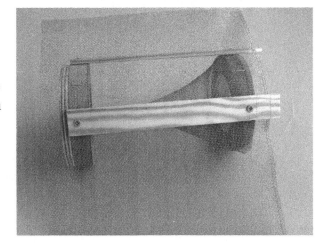

10. Roll the trap and wrap the mesh - stapling as you go and fixing a leg at each set of quarter marks. Mesh will overlap, ensure you staple the overlap.

11. When you get all the way round, you'll be back to the first leg that you temporarily attached to the rings. Remove this leg, overlap the ends of the mesh and staple it in place. Now refix the trap leg permenantly in place.

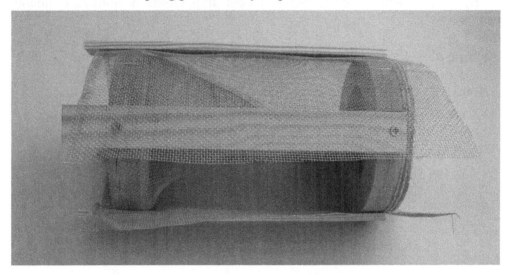

In Use

To use the trap it needs to be baited underneath and bait should be placed in a small, shallow dish – an upside down jam jar lid is ideal.

In their original instructions for the 'Sur-Katchem' trap, Olsens & Sons recommend the following baits:

- Spring blow flies – a piece of fish, meat or part of any dead animal.

- House flies – pickle juice, vinegar and sugar.

Chapter 10 – The Crayfish Trap

The last of our Funnel Trap projects is probably one which is recognisable to most people – who hasn't seen a lobster pot when visiting the seaside? The freshwater crayfish is a distant cousin of the lobster and has been found in British waters for thousands of years, although now in decline. One of the main reasons for their reducing numbers is the spread of the larger, more aggressive and non-indigenous Signal Crayfish.

It's a familiar story of foreign animals brought to the UK for commercial or ornamental purposes, (e.g. mink, muntjac deer, grey squirrel), which have then escaped and thrived to the detriment of many native species.

Because our native species are under such pressure the trapping of Crayfish in the UK requires an authorisation, issued by the Environment Agency. This is free and comes with an extremely useful and practical information pack. The authorisation ensures that anyone trapping crayfish is doing so responsibly, has the right information to identify crayfish species and is <u>using a trap which is safe</u> and will not pose a risk to other river wildlife. It is also strongly recommended that you obtain the landowner's permission.

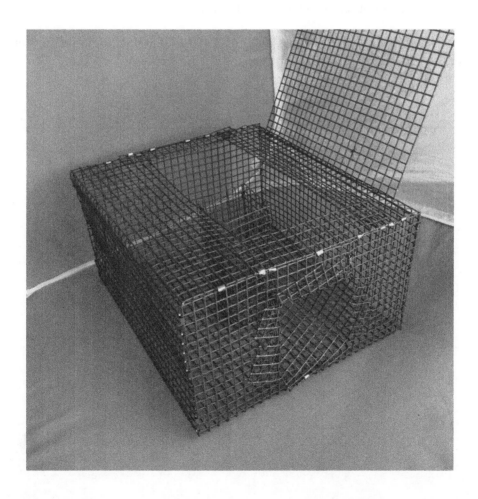

The easiest way to obtain the application form is via the Environment Agency website, but paper copies of the guidance booklet and application forms are available by email at enquiries@environment-agency.gov.uk or by phone on 0370 8506506. As far as making your own trap is concerned you'll need to make sure that it is suitable and matches the guidelines laid down by the Environment Agency.

Any trap that you make will need to be approved by the Agency as part of your authorisation application.

The ground rules for any trap are:

- The entrance to the trap must be no more than 9.5 cm across.

- If the entrance is more than 9.5 cm across, there must be an otter guard or restriction on the funnel leading into the trap.

- The holes in the mesh must not be more than 3 cm across.

- The trap itself must not be more than 60 cm long or 35 cm wide.

The plans in this chapter have been reviewed by the agency and found to be in line with these published guidelines and not requiring an Otter Guard.

However if you should ever need to make an Otter Guard, there are some recommended approaches in the Environment Agency information.

Cutting List & Materials

Mesh

Don't be tempted to use mesh that is too weak and thin. A flimsy trap will soon bend out of shape, the doors will no longer close tightly and using it will become very frustrating. Even if you don't think you have otters in your area, there's a good chance that you'll have mink and certainly rats. Your trap needs to be strong enough to withstand the interest of these predators.

19 gauge is just not up to the job and you should use at least 14 or 12 gauge mesh.

The guidelines limit the maximum mesh size to 30mm, but I'd recommend squares of 20mm or smaller which helps with the rigidity of the trap. The funnels need to be smaller as explained later.

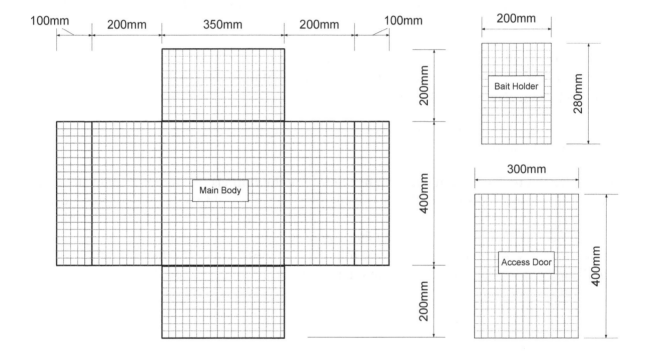

Cord & Weights

You're also going to need a good length of strong, rot proof cord to be able to pull the trap back to land. You may also want some weights to hold the trap securely on the river bed, although the weight of the trap might be enough. Any extra ballast doesn't need to be terribly heavy and whatever you use you'll need to be able to secure them to the base of the trap.

The Funnels

The shape, rigidity and secure fixing of the funnels are all key to the success and safety of this trap. You do not want your captured crayfish to escape but more importantly you must not allow any non-target animal to get stuck in the trap and drown. Crayfish are a tasty food for most marine mammals and if your trap is successful, then a cage full of them is likely to attract a lot of attention.

As has been explained earlier the small end of your tunnel must be no wider that 95mm. So for a circular tunnel that's the diameter, but if you use square tunnels then they must be 95mm or less corner to corner.

With a bit of basic trigonometry we can see that the small opening of our funnel needs to be NO LARGER than 67mm by 67mm. Remember that you can always make the smaller if you wish.

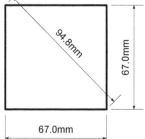

Another advantage of this plan is that you can make various pairs of funnels, of different sizes. You can try them all out in your cage and see which you have most success with.

The measurements in the following steps will create a funnel 70mm deep, with a wide opening approx 113mm by 113mm and a narrow opening approx 55mm by 55mm.

I strongly suggest that you do a dummy run of this using a piece of card or stiff paper, before you try it with mesh.

You will need to use a mesh with smaller holes for the funnels – 10mm x 10mm squares at the largest but smaller is better. If you use anything larger you'll find that the squares create large 'steps' where you make the cuts and this will give a jagged opening of unpredictable size. For this reason I also recommend that you make the opening of the funnel smaller than you ultimately want as the manufacturing tolerances in mesh could alter the size quite significantly. It's relatively easy to trim it larger after the funnel is folded.

Varying the Funnel Size.

The depth and size of the small opening can be changed by simply adjusting the measurement of the small arc. There's a bit of trigonometry that works all this out, but essentially the length of one side of the small opening will be the length of the small arc multiplied by 0.7653. I recommend that you begin with a middle sized funnel of small arc 70mm and adjust from there.

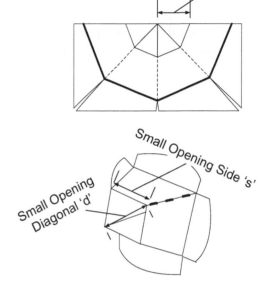

Length of small Arc	Side of small opening	Diagonal of small opening
87mm	67mm	94mm
80	61mm	87mm
70	54mm	76mm
60	46mm	65mm
50	38mm	54mm

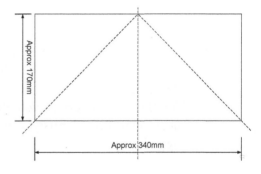

Making the Funnels

1. Cut a rectangler mesh approximately 170mm by 340mm. As with all mesh projects work to complete squares and in this instance make sure the long side is an even number of squares long.

2. Using a straight edge and a marker pen, divide the rectangle into two equal squares. Then into four triangles as shown.

3. Measure along both the diagonals, the midline and edges a distance equal to the length of the short side, less about 20mm. Mark all these 5 points.

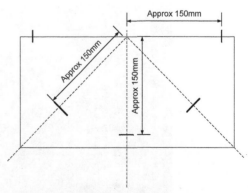

4. Join these points as shown to form an arc.

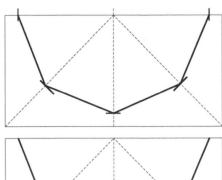

5. Make cuts in the mesh from the outside edge up to the arc that you've drawn. This creates a series of four 'flaps' around the edge.

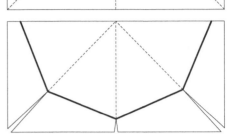

6. Repeat steps 3 and 4 to create a smaller arc

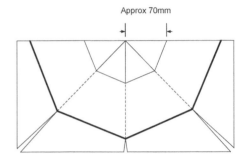

7. And then cut out the small section. This will become the opening of your funnel.

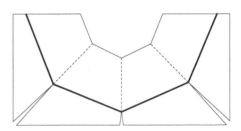

8. Using a strong, straight edge, bend these flaps upwards. Bend them along the edged of the marked arc.
   The flaps will overlap each other where they meet. Don't be surprised if it looks a bit ragged.

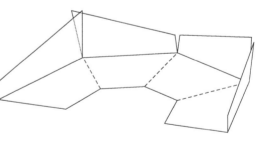

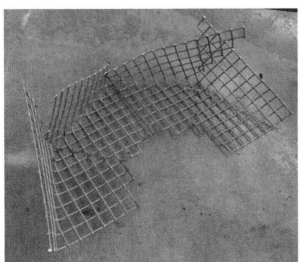

9. Bend the four sections of the funnel together, again using a strong straight edge and secure the join with cable clips. Make sure that there is a clip near the funnel opening to prevent it being forced wider.

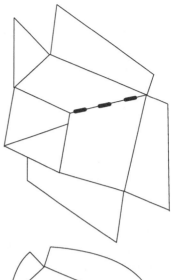

10. Finally trim the flaps making sure that you leave enough to secure the funnel onto the cage.

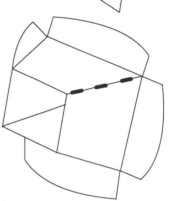

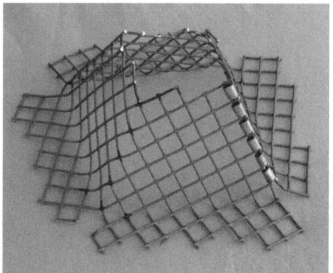

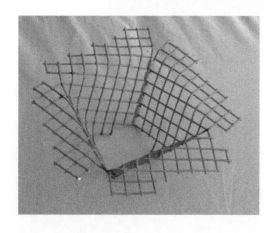

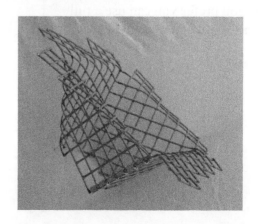

Folding & Fixing the basic cage

Once your funnels are made, mark and cut two holes in the side walls of the main cage.

The holes should be just big enough for the funnel to fit into but the flaps on the funnel should stop it going all the way through.

I prefer to place the funnels in the short sides so that they are the maximum distance apart.

You don't have to use two funnels or place them as shown here. The trap featured in the photo at the start of this chapter is a single funnel model.

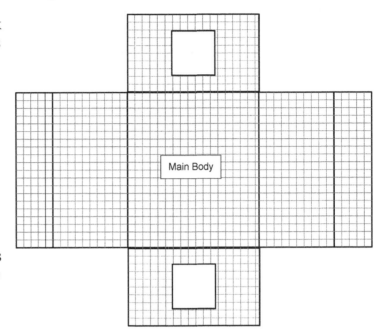

Use the Mesh Bender or an alternative method, to fold the sides and the top of the trap together.

In this plan the opening in the trap top runs the full length of the trap, but if you prefer you can use a full top and simply cut out an entry hole.

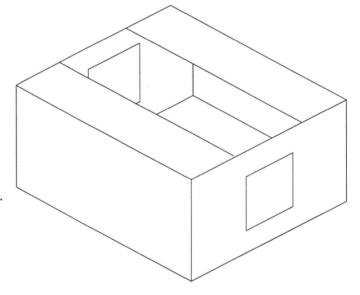

Bait holder and lid

The lid should be positioned so that it overlaps the opening on both sides and then fixed on one edge to form a hinge. When closed the door need to be held in place firmly either using spring locks, cable ties or even both.

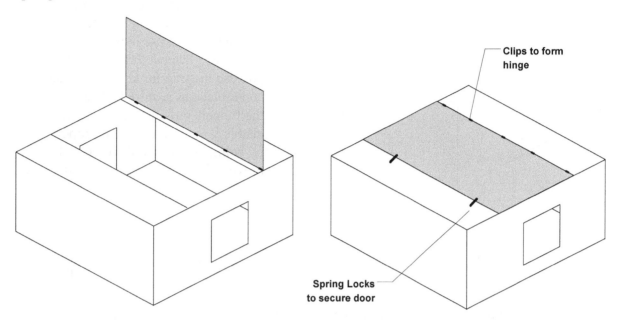

The mesh layout at the start of this chapter includes an idea for a bait holder. In practice you don't need one of these or you can simply use a mesh bag tied inside the cage, but I think this adds to the simplicity of the trap. The mesh is bent into a hollow square tube and fastened along the joint. The length of this tube is the same as the height of the cage, so if stood upright and fixed to the floor of the cage, the door of the cage will double as a door to the bait holder. When emptying the trap it takes seconds to refill with bait while the door is open.

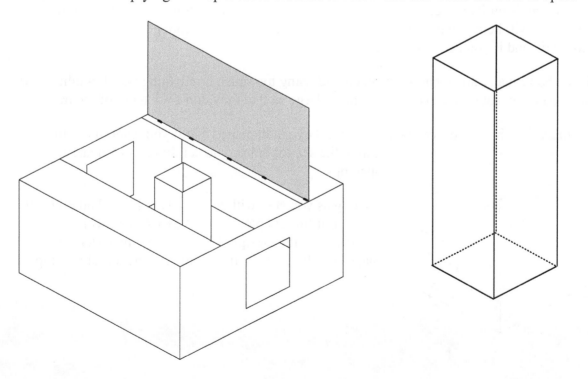

Fitting the Funnels

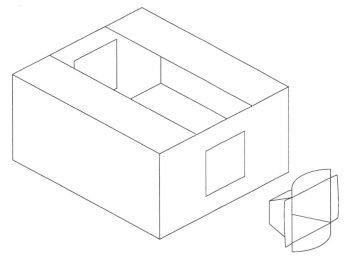

Inset the funnels from the outside of the cage and secure with clips. On small holed mesh you may not be able to fit the pliers through so an alternative is to use lock wire AND cable ties. Inspect these every time you use the trap for signs of damage and replace as required. The flaps on the funnels provide a good overlap to enable you to secure them properly and by being larger than the hole, help to prevent the funnel being pushed inside.

In Use

Attach your cord to the top of the trap at several points – joining together at the main line. This will help you to pull the trap out level and is also a safety feature in case one of the tie on points comes free.

As much as possible lower the trap in and lift it out vertically.
This is not always going to be easy, or even possible, but dragging the trap along the river bed is just likely to damage it or get it tangled in the weeds.

Once the trap is built and secured to a line, have a few practices getting it in and out of the water. This will help you get a sense of whether the cord is strong enough, whether it's tied on correctly and if you need to add any weights.

Bait can be virtually any meat scraps but avoid using too much or anything which might contaminate the water. Keep the pieces fairly large so that they don't wash out of the trap.

Remember that the funnels can be renewed if they get damaged and if you want to use the trap in the sea for crabs, you can fit ones with larger openings.

As long as you stay within the Design Rules laid down at the start of this chapter why not experiment with variations on this design ? Try different materials or shapes for the funnels, try a funnel in the top of the trap.

Chapter 11 – Side Entry Corvid Traps

A common request we receive is for plans to make a Side Entry Larsen style trap. Traditionally side entry traps have been made by simply moving the door to the side and converting it to a sideways 'swing in' style. However during my research I have come across several alternative designs for side entry doors which are very practical and easy to make.

In this chapter I have not provided one simple plan to follow but instead explained how these different doors work and some of the ways in which they can be built. This will give you the flexibility to make your own traps with whichever types of door you want. They can be used on a mesh Larsen trap and just as easily on the conventional wood and wire style.

Although the mesh Larsen is really nothing more than a large box with dividers, I have also taken the opportunity to suggest ways to make that basic structure.

The law which allows the use of live decoys in this way carries with it significant and serious responsibilities. The use of Larsen Traps to catch corvids is permitted under WCA 1981 through General Licences. All relevant animal welfare legislation must be complied with at all times, including the Animal Welfare Act 2006 which states that you must not cause unnecessary suffering to the call bird.

In practical terms this translates to daily checks to:
- ensure that the decoy bird has adequate food, water at all times, a suitable perch that does not cause discomfort to the bird' feet and appropriate shelter (located above the perch). Where inclement weather (hot or cold) is forecast, consideration should be given to providing further shelter for the decoy or removing the decoy altogether.
- deal with any catches
- to release non-targets unharmed (if appropriate to do so)
- NOTE: In Scotland Larsen traps must now be registered and be labelled with a unique identification number.

Any injured call bird must be dispatched quickly and humanely. It is good practice to replace the call bird regularly. Dispatch methods are discussed in chapter 13.

Whatever you make from these plans, you must ensure that part of the Call Bird Compartment is covered over, that it contains a perch for the call bird and that there is adequate food and water.

A very good idea for providing water is to use any 75cl plastic drinks bottle with a segment cut out of the side which helps to prevent the call bird from fouling the water. This can be secure to the wire mesh with a couple of plastic cable ties.

Side Entry Door Designs

Fitting the Trap Doors follows the same process described in fitting the access hatch – except that the doors and the holes are larger and in the front of the call compartments.

The exact details will depend on the type of door that you decide to use.

Conventional Door

The key thing to remember here is that opposite to the top-entry design, the door needs to swing inwards not outwards. You will not have gravity working with you to 'drop' the bird down into the box so you're relying on the door to 'sweep' it in. Many people choose to use a 'bungee cord' style spring instead on this sort of door as a conventional cage spring can be used but requires a bit more skill.

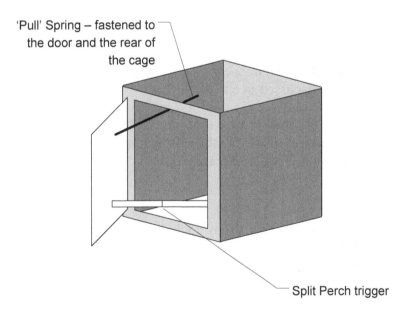

'Pull' Spring – fastened to the door and the rear of the cage

Split Perch trigger

When fitting the door it's best to leave at least two clear rows of mesh all around the hole that you create.

The door should be one row bigger than the hole - all the way round. Remember that's a row on every side so the door will need to be 2 rows taller and wider than the hole.

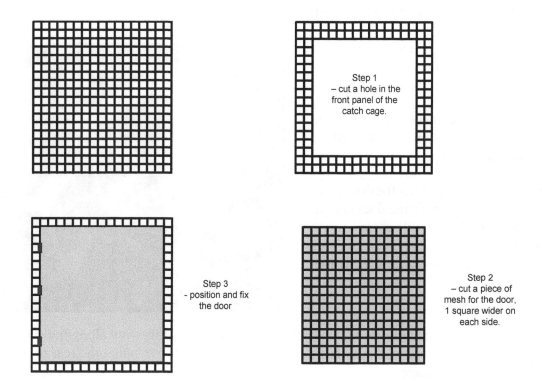

Step 1
– cut a hole in the front panel of the catch cage.

Step 2
– cut a piece of mesh for the door, 1 square wider on each side.

Step 3
- position and fix the door

The Importance of a good hinge

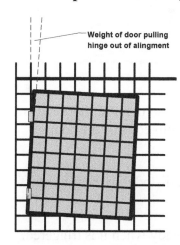

Weight of door pulling hinge out of alingment

The other factor critical to the success of this door design is the quality of the hinge. The weight of the door will be pulling downwards with a lever effect on the hinge. Combined with the force of the spring, any slackness is likely to cause the door to move out of alignment and possibly not close properly or quickly enough. This is worst where you're using clips or rings that are completely free to move around – not normally an issue on top hinged doors.

As a general rule use multiple contact points along the hinge and don't just rely on one or two clips. Get them as tight as you can without causing the door to stick.

In these diagrams the effect is exaggerated to demonstrate the issue. The ideal would be to have one side of the 'hinge' is fixed and only one side free to move. For example by welding one side of each clip or by using loops made from the wire of the door itself, as described in Chapter 13.

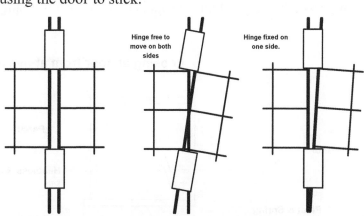

Hinge free to move on both sides

Hinge fixed on one side.

Conventional Door - Wooden Frame

For this style of door it is worth sharing a few extra tips about the best approach when using a wooden frame.

You can, of course, make it just the same as the wire mesh version, with the split perch outside the trap.

However the way in which the doors are mounted on a wooden frame does enable you to do something a little more sophisticated. By moving the spring and the axle of the door away from the corner you can make a rather clever change to the trigger.

The trick is to move the pivot point and spring about a quarter of the way along the door. This doesn't reduce the size of the opening too greatly, but does mean that the rear of the door now pivots *inside* the cage.

A trigger can now be employed which makes use of the tension between this rear edge and the side of the cage. The trigger uses a single length of perch with a pin or headless nail inserted a little way along. This distance should be just less than the distance between the pivot and the short end of the door.

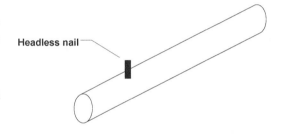

When the door is opened fully the trigger can be placed inside the trap so that the short end is against the inside wall of the cage and the pin just catches on the bottom edge of the door. This will hold the door open.

The weight of any bird landing on the perch will push it downwards, dislodging the pin from behind the door and allowing the door to swing closed.

A great advantage of this design is that the bird is <u>inside</u> the cage already when it is triggered.

Looking at door from above in set position

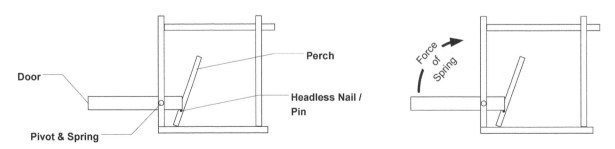

These photos are of a scale model Larsen Trap, built for demonstration purposes, and show the mechanism in set position.

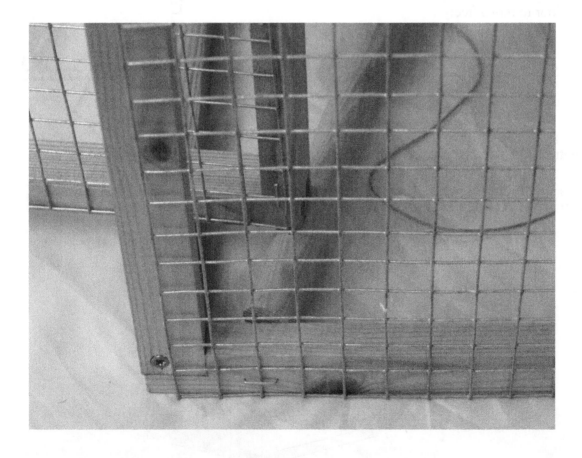

Top Hinged Door

The second option for a side opening trap is to borrow from traditional cage trap design. In this arrangement the door is swung from the top so gravity is working with us and there is no concern about amount of force being placed on a side hinge. This style of trap has been very successful in the control of Grey or Hooded crows in Ireland and uses a very simple spring powered, top hinged door.

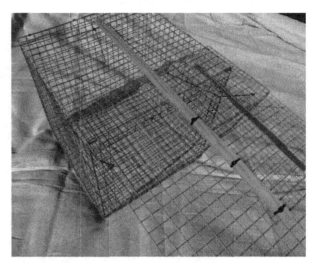

Make the door and the cage opening the same as for the conventional door, **except that the door needs to be slightly longer.** You need two clear rows of mesh all around the hole **plus the extra length to reach the top edge of the cage**.

The door is hinged from the top and right on the top edge of the cage where the front and the cage roof meet. The door needs to be able to open so that it's flat and level with the cage roof. Make the hinge using loosely fitted cage clips or cable ties; not so loose that the door wobbles about but enough slack for the door to move freely.

Ideally the door should be sprung so that it closes quickly and stays shut. A coil spring on the hinge or a pull spring inside the trap will both work well, but

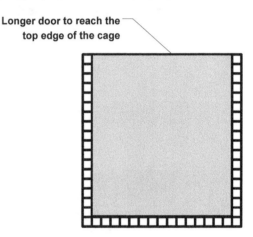

Longer door to reach the top edge of the cage

make sure that it's off to the side and doesn't interfere with the bird entering the trap.

The trigger rod is a straight length of metal rod or even wooden dowel which is fixed down the centre of the door. It needs to be long enough to reach the trigger mechanism at the back of the trap and also a good way down the length of the door. A good tip on the first trap you make is not to fix this until you have fitted the trigger as the position of the end of the rod is critical!

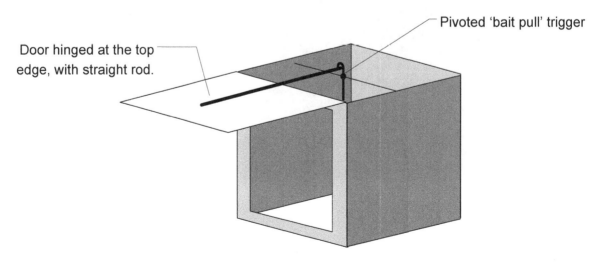

Door hinged at the top edge, with straight rod.

Pivoted 'bait pull' trigger

The trigger on this trap is a variation of the 'bait pull' principle described in Trap Making Step by Step. Essentially a small lever which at the top hooks just over the end of the Trigger Rod. The lower end of the lever is baited and when the bait is pulled the lever moves; releases the rod and the door. How you go about implementing this in practice is up to you and there are many options you can choose from.

Wire Rod Trigger

Any trigger needs to be strong enough so as to move when pulled and not just flex. High tensile wire can be suitable as it's designed to be rigid but that can make it quite hard to work. The trigger needs to have a pivot point near the top end – how near will depend on where you mount the pivot on the cage and how low down the Door Rod comes when the trap is set.

Two methods can be used to create this pivot point – either a tight loop or coil in the trigger itself or a small nut welded onto it.

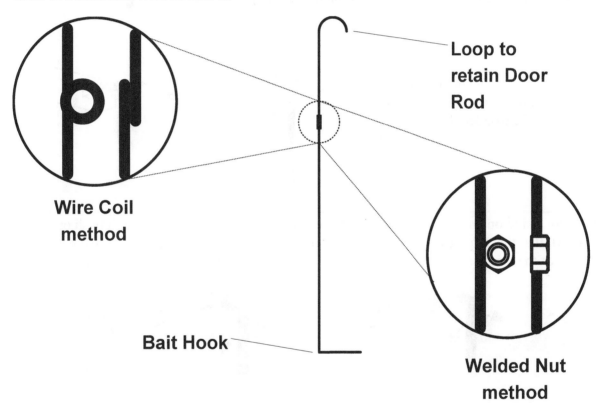

Wire Coil method

Loop to retain Door Rod

Bait Hook

Welded Nut method

Trigger Mounting

In all cases the trigger needs to be pivoted at or near the top of the cage. This can be done as simply as attaching it to the mesh top with a loose cable tie and relying on the power of the sprung door to hold everything in place.

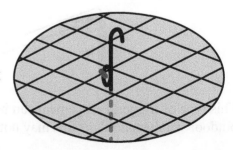

A better option, which doesn't take much more effort, is to use a short length of rod placed through the pivot loop of the trigger and then attached to the top of the cage with drilled blocks, clips or cable ties. This method allows the trigger to move freely and smoothly which can require less of a pull on the bait.

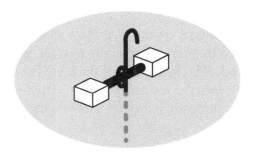

Trigger / Rod Engagement

Again the easiest method can be seen in the first Trigger Mounting photograph on the previous page. Simply looping the top of the Trigger over the end Rod so that a good tug on the bait will cause it to slip off and release the door. The downside of this method is that any 'push' on the baited trigger will actually have the opposite effect and will move the Trigger further up the Rod making the trap less likely to go off.

This can easily be countered by fitting a 'collar' to a metal Rod or making a notch in the end of a wooden Rod

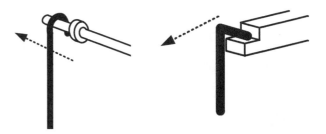

By using a side-on engagement you can create a trigger that will fire on either a push or a pull. All that this requires is an extra bend in the end of the Trigger and a 90 degree bend in the end of the Rod, or the addition of a small 'ledge' welded on to the side of the Rod.

In the case of a wooden Rod a small block of wood or even just a couple of oval headed nails.

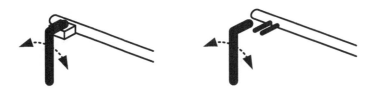

This type of trigger arrangement can be built so that the trap can be set very fine, but in outdoor windy conditions this may not be advisable.

Powering the Door

Even though this door swings down under its own weight, it would be unwise to rely on this to keep the door closed tightly enough to prevent the birds escaping. You could add a locking mechanism, similar to that described in Chapter 13, but in most cases it's simpler to add some kind of spring.

'Bungee'

Quick, simple and cheap, the 'bungee' elastic strap is always popular and has the advantage that it can quickly and easily be replaced. Most people will be familiar with these for strapping things down to car roof-racks or trailers. However it is easy to buy smaller, thinner bungee straps from many camping shops and even to buy cord on a reel so that you can cut your own to length. You can even use a pair of these, one either side, to ensure a strong and tight closure.

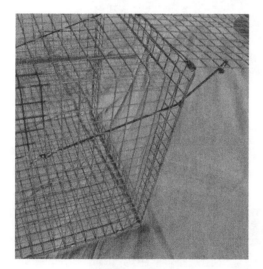
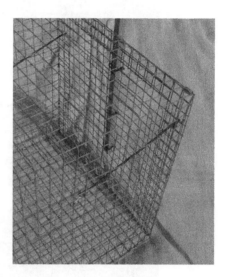

When attaching the bungee make sure that it's well out of the way and does not obstruct the entrance. Also check that it's still pulling tight even when the door is closed.

Bungee cords usually come with a hook fixed to each end, which can interfere with the closing of the doors. I usually remove the hook and attach the cord directly to the door by wrapping it through the mesh and clipping it in place.

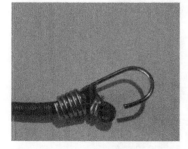

A long coiled spring works the same way as a bungee and can be used instead.

This is a very effective Hooded Crow trap which was the inspiration for this section. It was made by Tomas Carrigy from Athboy in Co. Meath, Ireland and was based on an original idea by Diarmuid Priest.

Guillotine Door

This door design was first shown to me by a trap making friend Keith who lives in France, where he has used the design very effectively. The idea of a Guillotine or Drop Door is of course very familiar but this was the first time I'd seen it applied to a bird trap. Like most of the best designs, the trigger mechanism is so simple that you will wonder why you'd not thought of it yourself. It combines the idea of a perch as the trigger and the traditional 'pull peg' release for a drop door.

Critical to this design is that the door must be able to slide freely and drop quickly and smoothly under its own weight. The slots or runners must also continue above the height of the trap a little way so that they still hold the door in line when it is propped in the open position. About a quarter of the doors height is about right.

The mechanics of the trap are based around the wire trigger – a framework of two rectangles connected opposite and at right angles to each other along a central axle or pivot. The ends of this pivot rail extend past the rectangles so that the ends can be mounted in the frame and allow the whole framework to rock back and forth

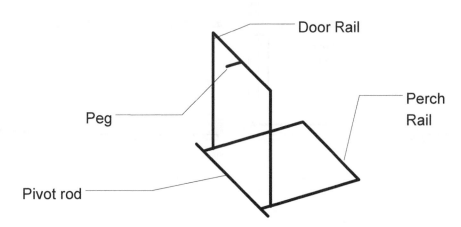

When positioned in the doorway of the trap, one rectangle (the Perch Rail) stick out into the body of the trap – level but held above the floor. The other rectangle (the Door Rail) stands vertical just inside the cage. At the top of the Door Rail there is a small peg which pokes back through the door way and supports the base of the door.

To set the trap, the door is slid upwards in the slots until fully open. The wire trigger can then be rotated towards the trap opening until the 'peg' is just under the opened door. This will also raise the 'perch' up from the floor of the trap. Holding the trigger in place, the door can be gently lowered until it rests on the 'peg' and then both parts will be held in place by each other.

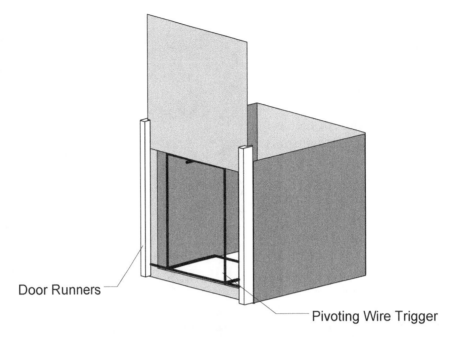

Door Runners

Pivoting Wire Trigger

When a bird enters the trap and perches on the Perch Rail, its weight pushes the rail downwards. This causes the whole trigger to rock forward on the Pivot Rod, moving the Door Rail further inside the cage and pulling the peg from under the door. This releases the door allowing it to slide down the runners and close the trap.

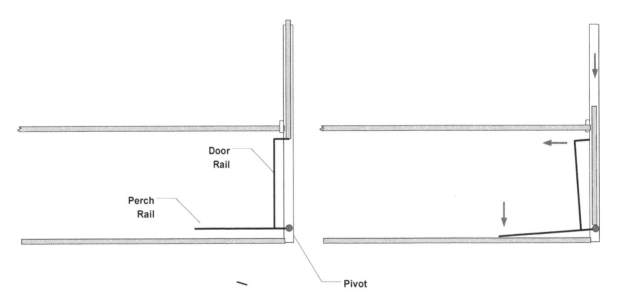

Door
Rail

Perch
Rail

Pivot

Making the Runners

Before you make the door you should make and dry fit the runners, or at least have planned them out against the cage so that you know how wide the door needs to be. The runners themselves are just a simple channel and don't need to be particularly strong. However they do need to be straight and not so thin that the slightest blow will knock them out of shape.

There are many options for making the runners including these ideas:

- Most DIY chains sell pre-formed channel in a variety of metals. A typical size has internal dimensions of 6mm wide by 10mm deep, which is ideal.

- If you have access to metal sheet and a suitably shaped former, you can create the same sort of channel yourself.

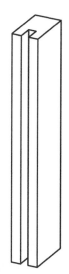

- You can use a router to cut out a straight channel from a length of seasoned hardwood.

- I've also heard of people using sliding rail for a shower door.

At the bottom of each runner you also need to create a mounting hole for the Pivot Rod. This can be as simple as drilling a hole through the back of the slot / channel, or you can fix an ordinary hex nut in place.

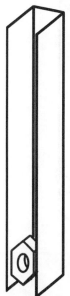

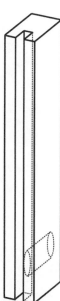

It's crucial that these mountings line up at the same height on both runners and are big enough to allow the Pivot Rod to move smoothly but not too loosely

The door will slide down the runners and rest on the Pivot rail when it drops after the trap is triggered.

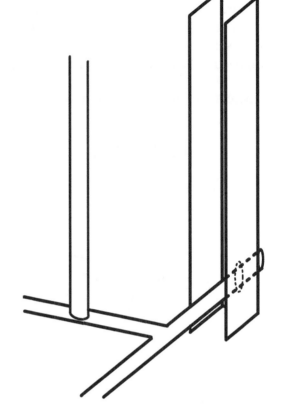

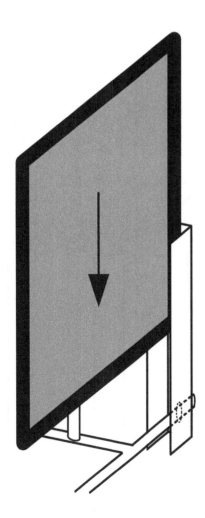

Attaching the Runners

How you attach your runners depends a little bit on the material that you've made them from. Wooden ones can be fixed with a couple of screws from inside the cage, using large washers if you're attaching to mesh.

Make sure that you've allowed enough depth in the runner to be able to screw into solid wood and not block the groove by mistake.

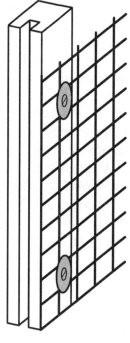

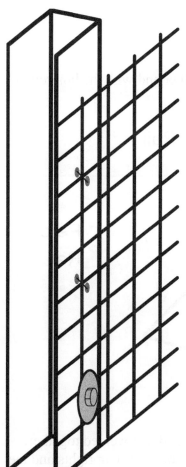

The simplest way to attach metal runners is to use a bolt at the base, but below where the door reaches when closed. Using bolts any further up will block the channel and the doors won't be able to run up and down.

Use lock wire a couple of times further up to hold the channel steady and in place.

Drill a couple of small holes next to each other and pass the lock wire through. Twist it over a strand of the mesh and use lock wire pliers to spin it tight. When you drill the lock wire holes remember that the two runners go on opposite side and so need to be mirror images of each other.

Alternatively you can of course you can always make bracket or spot weld them in place.

Whichever method you use remember to keep testing with the door to make sure that it opens and closes without any problems.

Doors

As with the previous designs, the door needs to be at least one clear row of mesh larger than the hole – all the way round. For this design I suggest that you allow yourself as much spare on the door as you can at the start, so that you can adjust it to suit the runners.

In fact the door does not have to be made of mesh at all. Metal plate or wood are equally effective provided that the edges are clean and smooth and the wood will not swell too much if it gets wet. If mesh is used then make sure that you go over both edges thoroughly with a file to remove any burr or sharp edges left from the cutting out.

Another key factor is to get the door flat and for the material to be rigid enough to stay in shape.

Trigger

The trigger is made from two squares of wire connected to each other and with the horizontal 'square, attached to an axle or 'pivot rod'.

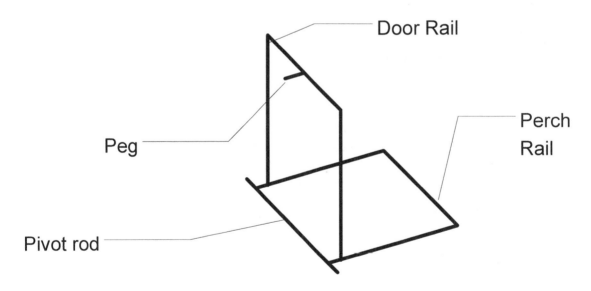

This can be made very simply using some 5 or 6 mm steel rod, shaped and welded together. This type of rod is commonly available from the major DIY superstores. The uprights and the Door Rail are positioned a little way along the horizontal bars leading to the Perch so that they don't get in the way of the dropping door.

Making the Bends

In order to get even, clean bends on the corners, I recommend making a very simple bending jig. A block of wood, (hardwood will last longer if you're going to be using it a lot), with a hole drilled right through and square to the top surface. The hole should be about 1mm larger in diameter than the rod that you want to bend, so that it can be pushed through easily, but still holds the rod tightly when you're bending it.

Clamp the bending jig securely in place and with enough room to be able to bend the steel rod.

Measure the length of one 'leg' of the one of the wire squares and mark the bend point on the length of rod. Hold the rod fairly close to the block and push it sideways and downwards, so that it begins to bend at the edge of the hole.

Continue pushing until the rod is bent at right angles.

Once bent and trimmed to size your pieces will be ready to weld together.

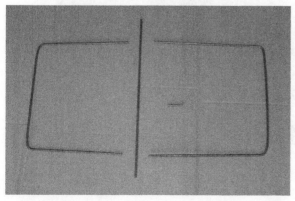
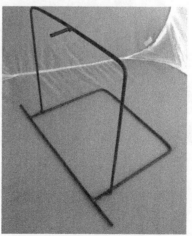

These are photos of Keith Hutton's original French Larsen Trap that was the inspiration for this door design.

The Mesh Larsen Cage

As explained in Trap Making Step by Step the Larsen Trap has two distinct sections; the holding cage for the call bird and the catch chambers for trapping the target birds. When making a wooden framed version it is almost always built as a single structure with internal dividers and that approach can also be taken with mesh built traps. However it is becoming increasingly popular to build the traps in individual sections, which gives much more flexibility in how the trap can be deployed. In this part of the chapter we'll look at both alternatives.

Materials, Tools & Equipment

The mesh size needs to be up to about ½ inch to 1 inch, (15 to 25mm). Use squares much bigger and any captives will be able to poke their heads through with possible injury; much smaller and it will be too dense and they won't go in. The mesh needs to strong enough to be able to maintain its own structure, 14 gauge or thicker. At a push you can use 16 gauge mesh and while the resulting cages will work, they will be quite delicate and so only suitable for experimental or very short term cages. Whatever mesh you use, you will also need cage clips to fasten the pieces together.

Cutting & Bending the Mesh

In the sections below measurements are given for mesh panels, bends and cut outs. Because mesh comes in different size and in different gauges of wire, take these measurements as a guide. Always work to complete squares of mesh when measuring whether it's going to be a bend or a cut. Unless it's very close indeed I always go slightly larger – that is out to the edge of the next complete square. If you're cutting the mesh remember to start your next measurement from the next complete square and don't count the one that you'll be cutting through. It's also critical that you are consistent in order for the different edges to line up correctly and be the same size.

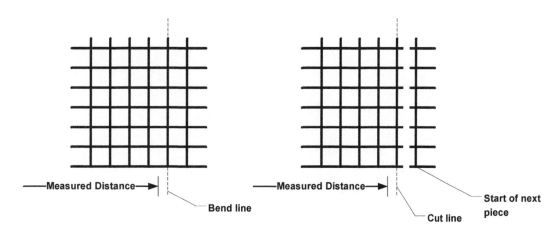

Making an 'all in one' cage

If you can get a piece of mesh large enough it's possible to make all of the outer cage from a single piece, but most people will be working with rolls that are 900mm or 36inches wide. With this conventional width it's possible to make the base, two sides and the top from a single piece, with just the dividers and two ends as separate pieces.

A little bit of planning can enable you to make the most efficient use of your mesh. The layouts given in this chapter should be taken as a guide but you'll see that even here there is some wastage. Spend a little time with a pencil and paper working out how best to fit the pieces into whatever mesh sheets or roll you obtain.

Personally I prefer to leave as much as I can in a single folded piece as I find it's easier to assemble when you have a sturdy, self supporting basic frame.

In practice you may prefer to cut all the sections out as individual pieces – the top, the base, four sides etc. This is a perfectly good method although you may find it a bit awkward attaching the first few pieces together.

Remember to measure this out in complete squares as explained above.

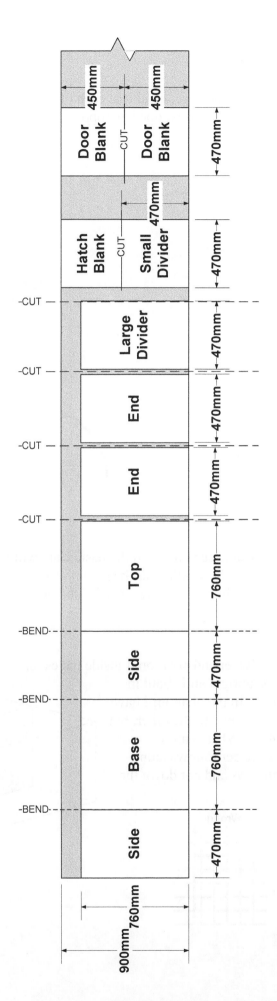

Making the Main Body

1. Take the largest section of the wire, bend it at each of the indicated lines as shown below to give you a rectangular box, open at opposite ends.

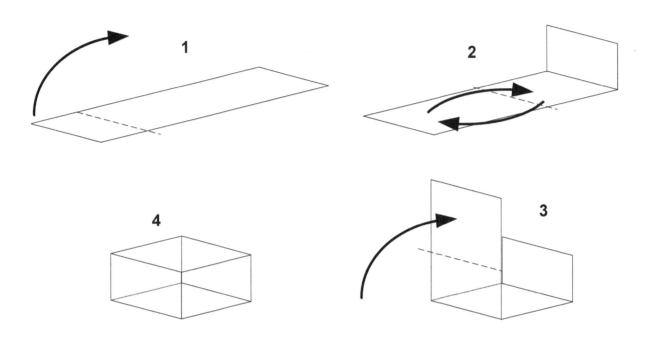

2. Secure the final edge using cage clips and the basic cage will look like this. In the following diagrams the shading has been removed so that the positioning of the internal dividers can be shown.

3. Next take the Large Divider and position it inside the cage. The divider should be upright and about in the middle of the cage. In the diagram I have it running from one open end to the other, but it doesn't really matter. What is more important is that the divider follows along the edge of the mesh rows and not down the centre of a square.

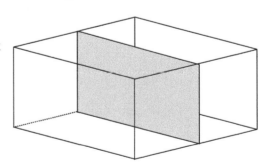

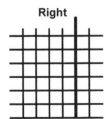

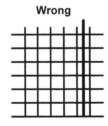

4. Next insert the small divider between one of the walls of the cage and the Large Divider. Again this should be central and along a mesh edge. If you have to make one side a square larger than the other that's fine.

    Secure with cage clips.

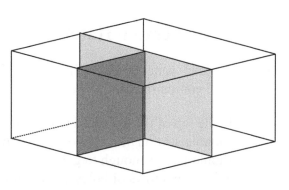

5. Finally take the two End Panels and secure them over the open ends.

    This completes the structure of the Larsen Cage.

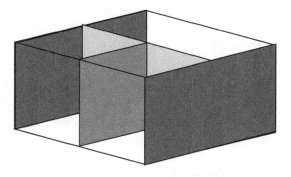

If you have **cut out all the pieces individually** then you should approach the assembly in a slightly different order. It will be easier to start with the base, build on two connected sides and then work your way around, before inserting the dividers and adding the top last of all.

Fitting the Service Hatch

In order to feed, water and care for the call bird, there must be an access hatch in the top of the call bird compartment.

1. In the top of the Call Bird Compartment, measure and mark a suitable section of mesh to remove to make the access hole. It should be big enough to get your hand through comfortably and at least two rows of holes away from any edge or divider.

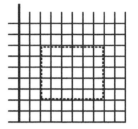

2. Take the Hatch Blank section of mesh and check that it is at least one row of holes larger than the hole you have marked. If not reduce the size of the hole to fit.

3. Trim and file the edges of the Hatch Blank to remove all sharp edges and burrs. This is now your Hatch Cover.

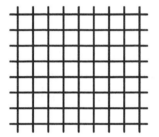 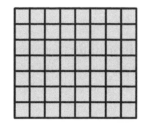

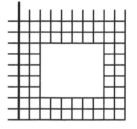

4. Check the sizes again before cutting the Access Hole that you had marked earlier. File away any sharp burrs.

5. Fit the Hatch Cover over the Access Hole using loose cage clips or cable ties to form a hinge and a suitable cage lock to secure it closed.

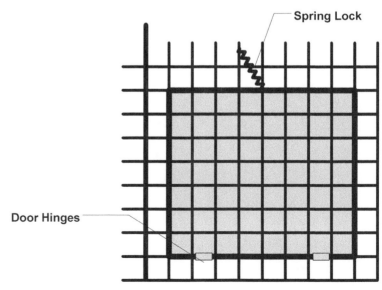

Making 'individual' cages

Why make the sections separate?

Making the call chamber and the catch boxes separately can have a number of benefits.

- To begin with it makes storage and transportation easier; an all-in-one trap is almost a meter square and half a meter deep. Being able to move this around in separate sections can be a significant advantage.

- Increased flexibility is another advantage and gives you a range of options on your trapping. You can use extra catch chambers if you're trapping a heavily populated area for the first time – just adding them round all four sides of the call bird chamber.

- You can swap different types of catch chamber depending on what's working at that location. Mixing top and side entry traps too.

- A caught bird can be taken away still inside its catch cage to be dispatched at a more appropriate location.

Call Bird Compartment

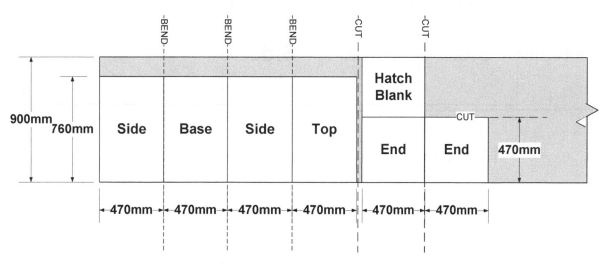

Remember to measure this out in complete squares as explained above.

Use the same method described for the 'all in one' cage to bend and build the final structure. Fit a service hatch in just the same way.

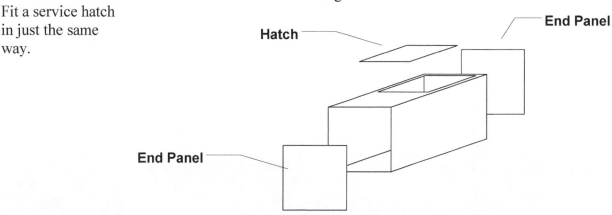

Catch Cage

The layout given below provides two 'U' shaped sections that fit into each other. This means that there are no loose individual sections of mesh to be attached and I think makes the whole structure more stable.

If you prefer you can cut the mesh into a number of other patterns – which ever you find easiest: (For example so that all the sides are connected and the top and base are individual pieces, or with top-side-base-side as a single piece with the two remaining sides as individual pieces.)

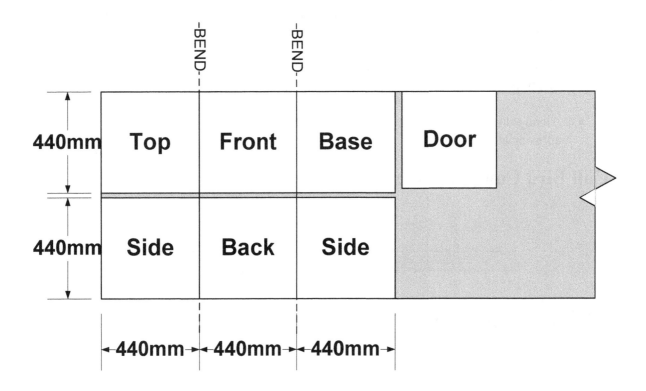

Assembly is again a simple matter of bending to shape and fixing.

Remember to measure this out in complete squares as explained above.

1. Take one of the cut sections and fold it to form a square 'U' shape.

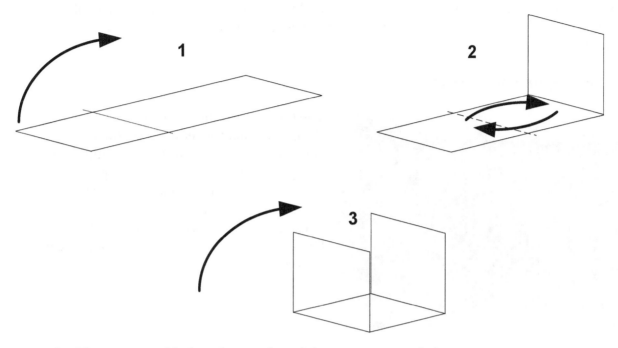

2. Then repeat with the other section giving you two equal shapes.

3. In one section cut the entrance for the catch chamber, before slotting the two halves together and securing with clips.

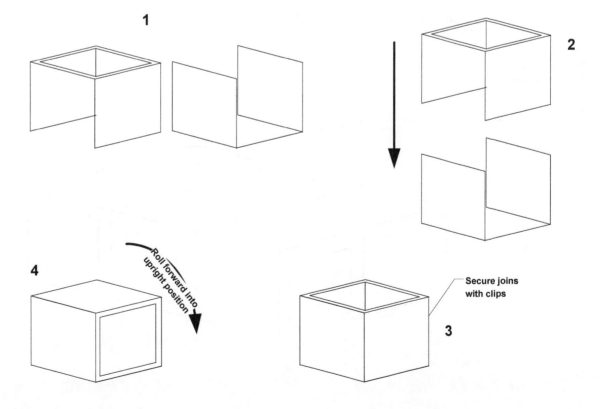

Other Variations on the Larsen Principle.

As with most cage traps, once you have understood the components there are a range of different ways in which you can combine them. These are a few more examples of overall structures.

A rectangular four catch

The trap that was the inspiration for the 'Drop Door' door and trigger has a central call bird compartment which runs the full width of the trap giving the call bird plenty of space to move about and stretch its wings as required by law. There are then four catch boxes, one in each corner, and set out as the diagram below so that each opens in a separate side of the trap.

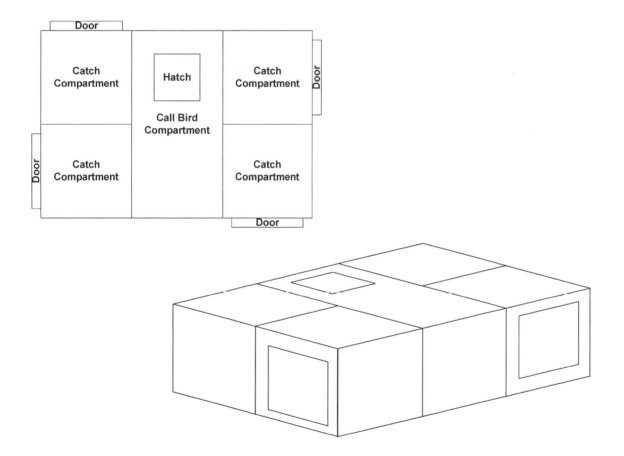

Circular

Popular in Australia and New Zealand this circular design completely surrounds the Call Bird Chamber to give 4 catch chambers.   In the UK any trap of this design needs to be made very large to satisfy the requirements for space and welfare of the call bird.

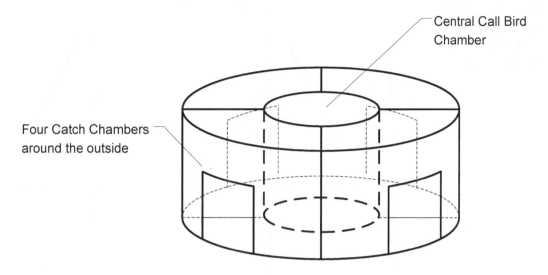

Central Call Bird Chamber

Four Catch Chambers around the outside

Larsen Mate

Not strictly a Larsen Trap, but a popular accessory is the recent 'Larsen Mate' or 'Clam' trap. This is a simple arrangement of matching cages of triangular section which are sprung so that they will close together when triggered.

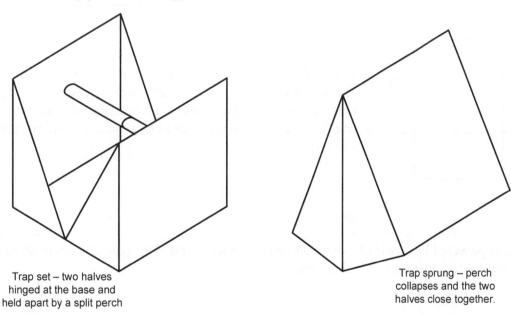

Trap set – two halves hinged at the base and held apart by a split perch

Trap sprung – perch collapses and the two halves close together.

At the time of writing there is some debate in the shooting press about the legality of these traps, based on a challenge made in Scotland. The reader is advised to check how this turned out before using any of these.

Making one of these is fairly straightforward, using 14g mesh of approximately 1 inch (25mm) squares.

Commercially made versions have genuine diagonal lines, with a wire welded along the edge to join up the loose edges of the cut squares.

Where this is not possible, the cutting of the mesh should be stepped to avoid cutting through part squares.

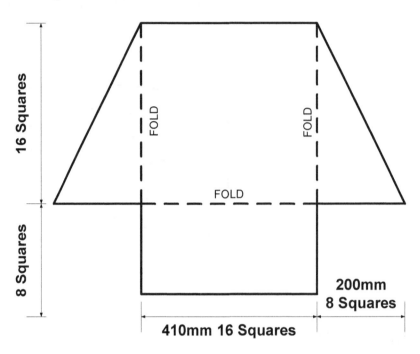

This will not provide such a neat or professional looking finish, but is unlikely to allow any birds to escape. Using mesh with smaller holes is also an option as this will give you smaller 'steps' but remember to still make the overall trap the same size.

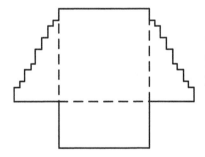

The trap is powered by a pair of extension springs or short 'bungee' type elastic, is set to pull the two halves together and keep them there.

SECTION 3

REVISITING
'TRAP MAKING, STEP BY STEP'

Since Trap Making Step by Step was published I have continued to collect new ideas and variations on those trap designs. Rather than producing a second edition, this chapter contains the best of this new information – the things which I would have included in Trap Making Step by Step if I'd known them when I wrote it.

More Trap Making – Step by Step

Chapter 12 – Pigeon Trap Improvements

For several years I have been involved in a long term Pigeon Trapping programme with one of the major UK pest control companies. This has given me an unprecedented opportunity to get feedback on its performance across a variety of locations and over a long operational period and to develop the trap design.

Improved Portability

The basic framework principle of the trap has remained the same – constructed of individual panels that can be bolted together on site. Crucially for this project the sections of the trap needed to be able to pass through small doorways and up tight stairwells which meant that the size of the panels needed to be reduced. They also needed to be as light as possible.

A key innovation was to replace the traditional heavy metal chicken wire and instead use commercial bird-proofing net. This tough nylon net is a subtler colour, weather proof, more flexible, less likely to harm a bird in a collision and above all much, much lighter.
The only downside was that with the weight of the assembled trap reduced, it was more prone to move in the wind. The addition of 'sandbag spurs' to the right hand corner of each frame resolved this problem.

While restricted access was a key factor in reducing the size of the trap, it wasn't the only one. Many roofs and service areas are exposed to high winds and where there is a parapet it's not usually any higher than 4ft. In an urban environment a shorter trap is much more discreet and less likely to catch the wind. The narrower width also made it practical to include a full width rail to carry the bobwire supports.

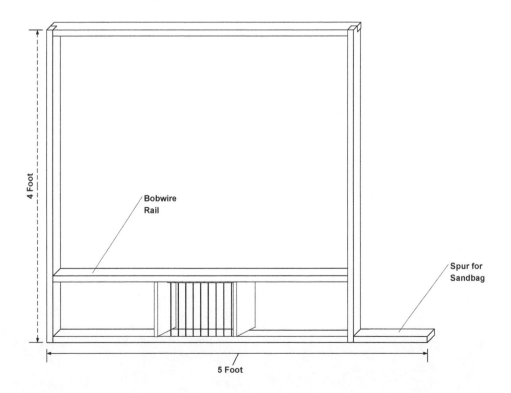

This left the problem of how to service the trap – clearly a 'walk in' design, but the low roof made it an awkward and uncomfortable task for the technicians involved.

The second major innovation was the introduction of the 'lift up' roof panel which gave the trap a temporary working height of 6 to 7 feet when required.

This was only possible because of the flexibility of the birdproof netting.

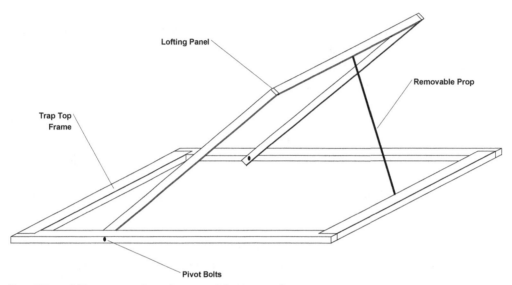

Roof Panel Framework – shown without netting.

Improved Retention

In common with some readers, we also had instances of captured pigeons squeezing their way out through bobwire doors. This was particularly the case with smaller young birds or feral racing pigeons familiar with loft structures.

Our third innovation was to make three simple changes to the trap entrances, which significantly reduced the number of escapees:

- The first thing is to cut the bobwires down to 7" or 9" in length. This is fairly easy to do with a pair of heavy duty wire cutters or a hacksaw. The metal is soft and cuts easily. These shorter bobwires remove some of the flexibility, but be sure to adjust the height of the frame to cater for the new length.

- The second improvement is to cut slots in the foot rail to correspond with the bottom of the bobwires. This means that when they are pushed outwards, the bobwires are effectively pinned at the bottom and not just at the top, but are still free to swing inwards.

- Even these changes will not prevent all escapes, particularly on an exposed windy site where the bobwire may be blown inwards allowing birds to slip under.

To counter this, I added ground funnels, another implementation of the 'Passive door' introduced in Trap Making Step by Step. These funnels can be very effective but require a flat and even surface to work properly – a corregated roof will allow birds to get back out.
By having both bobwire doors and funnels the trap had the flexibility to cope with most situations.

These are very easy to make using a small section of wire mesh and a pair of clips, or similar ties.

Making a Pigeon Trap Funnel

Mesh can be quite light weight but may suffer from being trodden on – by you and even by the pigeons if it's too thin!

14 or 16 gauge is about right.

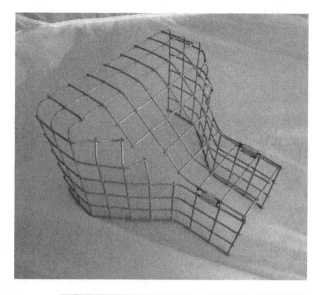

1   Obtain a piece of 1 inch mesh, 19 squares long by 9 squares wide.

2   Take a pair of good quality wire cutters, suitable for the thickness of mesh you're using. Cut along the lines indicated and remove the two scrap pieces. Be careful to cut on the 'scrap' side of the wires and leave the squares whole on the section you're going to use.

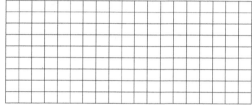

3   Discard the two scrap pieces.

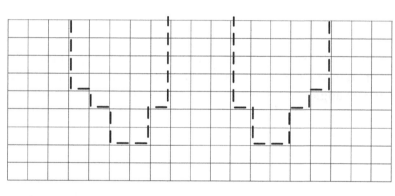

4   Using a hand file or small electric grinder smooth off any sharp burrs from where the mesh has been cut. Pay particular attention to the areas marked on the diagram as these edges will need to fit closely together.

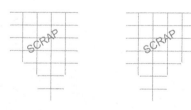

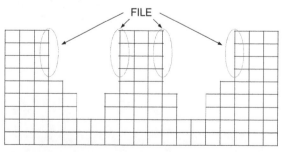

5   Using a mesh bender
    or a straight edge,
    make the first bend
    across all three parts
    of the wire as
    indicated. Bend all
    three legs, upwards
    at an angle of
    approximately 45 degrees.

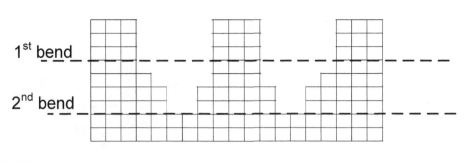

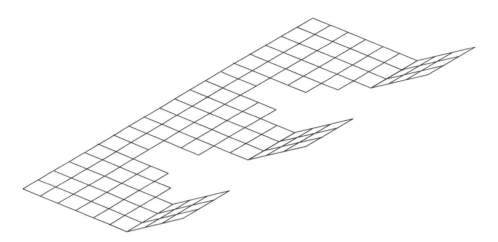

6   Flip the mesh over so that the bent sections are pointing downwards – it may help to hang them over the edge of the bench.   Now make the second bend **again upwards** and at the same angle

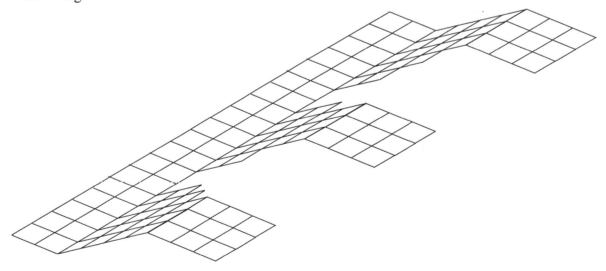

More Trap Making – Step by Step

7   The final bends bring the two sides in to form the three sided funnel.

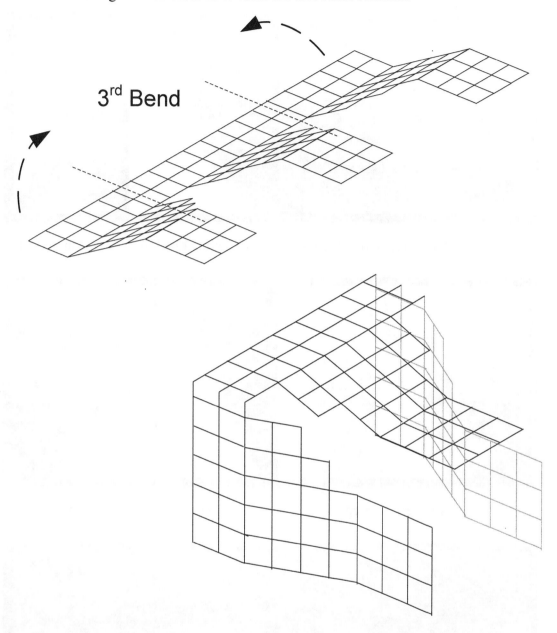

3rd Bend

8   The final step is to squeeze the loose sections of the funnel together and secure with a couple of cage clips.

Photo Steps

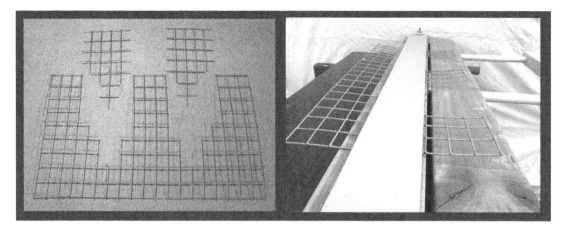

Pieces Cut and prepared at Step 4   Loading the blank into the mesh bender.

The first bend at Step 5   The second bend at Step 6

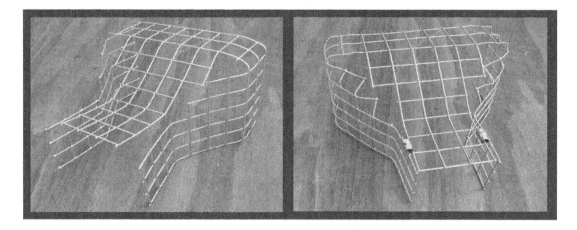

Bend into final shape – Step 7   Secure with clips – Step 8.

Chapter 13 –
More on Cages, Doors & Other Ideas
Sprung Cage Doors

One of the questions I have been asked by aspiring trap makers is 'How do you mount a spring to create a sprung door?' These photographs show an example of the method used on some classic cage traps manufactured by FENN and YOUNGS. The principles of the method are detailed on the following page.

1   On the top edge of the cage door trim the mesh by removing the crosspieces of the last row, to leave a short length of wire sticking out. Bend it over into a loop.

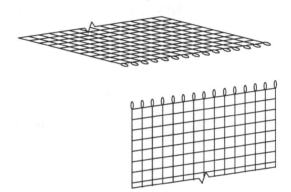

2   Do the same for the top of the door and the end of the cage roof.

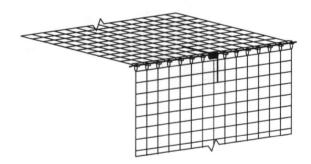

3   Bring together, overlap the loops and run a wire through as an axle.

Mount the spring on the same wire.

Swing-In vs. Swing-Out

The way in which you mount the spring does vary slightly, depending on whether you are making doors that swing from inside the cage, or that swing shut from the outside.

'Swing Out' Door

The door is folded inside the cage when set.

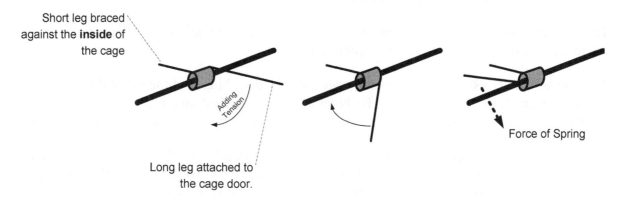

Short leg braced against the **inside** of the cage

Adding Tension

Long leg attached to the cage door.

Force of Spring

'Swing In' Door

The door is held outside the cage when set and swings closed against the outside.

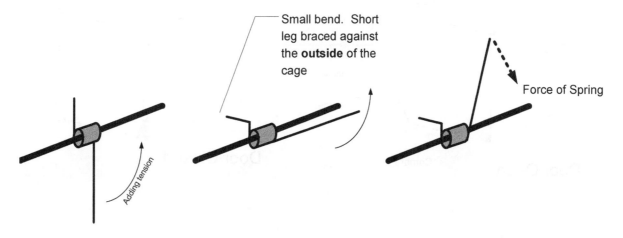

Adding tension

Small bend. Short leg braced against the **outside** of the cage

Force of Spring

Door Locks & Stops

In Trap Making Step by Step I introduced several different types of triggers and doors that can be used on cage and box traps. I also covered some of the locks and stops that could be used to make these doors more secure. In this section I've added a few more door lock ideas that can be used as alternatives.

Swing-Out Door - stop corners

This is such a simple and effective method of locking a 'Swing Out' door that it seems so obvious, but I'd not seen it in use until quite recently.

The trap is built as a standard rectangular cage with the door hinged at the top and free to swing back and forth at the opening. By blocking across the bottom corners of the cage, (with the door pushed inside first), the door is prevented from swinging all the way outwards.

For mesh traps the corners can be blocked using a single strand of thick wire looped between a square on the side and a square on the base. An alternative for wooden or metal panel traps is to fix a triangular plate across the corner – but really either method will work fine for both types.

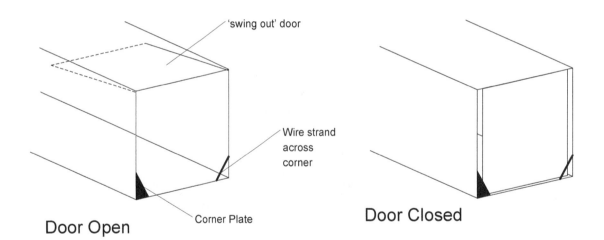

'swing out' door

Wire strand across corner

Corner Plate

Door Open

Door Closed

Swing-In Door– Falling Bar Lock

Similar to the 'Drop Bar' shown in Trap Making Step by Step, this is another lock for the outside of a 'swing-in' door.

A heavy rod or bar is mounted on vertical, parallel runners so that it can move freely up and down – most importantly so that it drops smoothly. Make sure that the holes drilled for the runners to pass through are big enough so that it won't stick.

With the door in the 'set' position the bar is held at the top of the runners, out of the way.

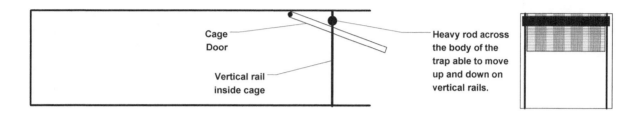

Cage
Door

Vertical rail
inside cage

Heavy rod across
the body of the
trap able to move
up and down on
vertical rails.

When the trap is triggered the door drops and the bar falls with it. The bar comes to rest against the outside of the door, very near to the bottom of the cage. Because of the angle of the door any pushing against the door from the inside pushes the rod sideways rather than upwards. To release simply lift the rod and the cage door can be opened.

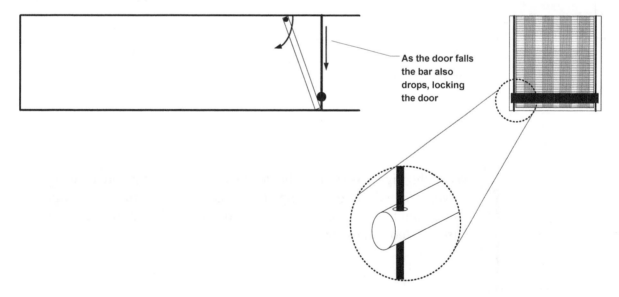

As the door falls
the bar also
drops, locking
the door

Drop Door – Falling Lever Lock

Gravity can also be used to lock a drop door, by making use of the channels that the door runs in. For this to work, the distance the door drops must not be any greater than the width of the door as the rod needs to fit in both directions.

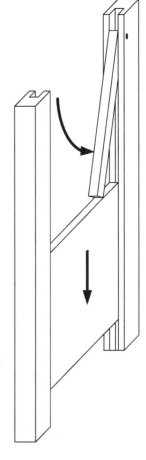

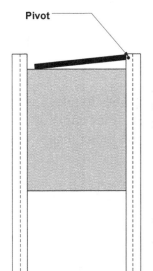

A square rod, slightly narrower than the thickness of the door, is pivoted inside one of the door runner slots.

When the door is in the raised and set position this rod rests across the top edge of the door.

When the trigger is sprung, the door falls, allowing the rod to swing down. When the door is completely closed the rod will hang straight down from the pivot and inside the door runner slot. Any attempt to raise the door is now blocked.

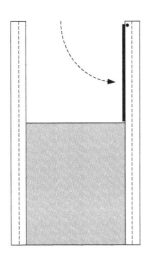

Dealing with catches

As mentioned in the introduction, it is critical that you, or someone else (e.g. farmer, gamekeeper), are able to deal confidently and competently with any successful live catches. If this is not the case, then live capture traps should not be set and advice should be sought from a professional pest controller. There have been a number of recent, high profile cases which have highlighted the legal and moral responsibilities for humane treatment of captured animals. I thought it worthwhile expanding on some of the tools and techniques available that can make this part of the process as efficient and effective as possible.

As a basic safety precaution gloves should be worn as rats, in particular, can carry potentially fatal diseases. Wherever possible you should avoid handling most animals altogether.

Cage Combs

A 12 ft/lbs-rated air rifle or 6 ft/lbs-rated air pistol (in .22 or .177 calibre) are recognised as efficient tools for the dispatch of rats, grey squirrels and even rabbits. With some species such as mink, consideration should be given to the use of steel-tipped Prometheus pellets. Even this requires careful shot placement to ensure a humane dispatch and that can be a challenge if the target animal is bouncing around inside the cage. The longer that goes on the more agitated both parties are likely to become.

One simple answer is to reduce the available space within the cage using a device known as a 'cage comb' or sometimes 'cage fingers', which can be made in several ways. One way is using single wire 'fingers' that are at least as long as the height of the cage and spaced out to match the holes in the mesh. These fingers are connected firmly across the top either by a welded bar or a wooden block.

An alternative design is a plywood sheet with slots cut into it to fit the cage wires.

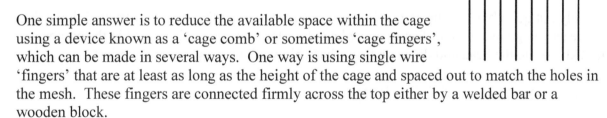

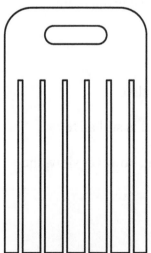

By approaching the cage from one end you will naturally encourage the trapped animal to move to the other. Reaching forward you can insert a cage comb through the top of the cage and through the mesh at the bottom, creating a temporary internal wall. It's worth having a pair of these because by changing your position you might get an opportunity to insert the second one and restrict movement even further.

Having reduced the available space, a short pause will allow things to calm down and enable you to take an easy and effective shot.

Priests and Poultry Dispatchers

Magpies and pigeons can be effectively and humanely killed by a sharp blow to the back of the head with a short, heavy stick known as a 'priest'. You should be holding the bird with one hand so that the blow is accurate and instant – it is not good enough to just swing at the birds and hope to hit them correctly.

Many farm suppliers sell a tool often called 'Dispatcher Pliers' or just 'Dispatchers' which are ideal for use in killing poultry on a small scale. They work by having a pair of overlapping jaws which, when applied to the neck of a bird, dislocate the spine instantly.

These are also widely used in the pest control industry for the humane dispatch of trapped feral pigeons and corvids.

Sack Method

For mammals, a simple way to make the 'sharp blow to the head' method more effective and more manageable is to add the use of a hessian sack. This needs to be a medium weight sack so that it's thick enough to contain the animal but not so thick as to cushion the blow. Though not as easy to find as they used to be, these sacks can sometimes still be obtained from independent pet shops that get peanuts delivered in them.

Release the rat or squirrel from the cage into the sack; twist the end closed and secure it either by put your foot on it, a heavy object or by using a large clip. But do it quickly.

Calmly but quickly work the animal into one of the corners of the sack, constricting down the space as you go using either feet or gloved hands. Once the animal is pinned in the corner, quickly locate the head and deliver a firm, sharp blow with a heavy stick or 'priest'.

The Importance of Checking

Whatever method you use, it is essential that whoever dispatches checks that the animal is dead. Many people talk about small movements after death being down to muscle reflex but many animals are quite skilled at 'playing dead' as a survival mechanism.

There are three 'signs' to look out for, and if in doubt, the animal should be given more attention.

The three signs are:

- Eye reaction – if the eye blinks when touched the animal is still alive.

- Pupil Dilation - if the pupils dilate with changing light the animal is still alive.

- Rhythmic breathing - if there is any signs of rhythmic movement, however slow, the animal is still alive.

Reader Suggestions

There are a few other ideas suggested by visitors to the website and well worth passing on.

Seesaw Trap Entrance

Adding an archway to the entrance of the seesaw trap has a number of benefits. It could be made from the same plywood as the body and with an opening in the lower half, 3 inches or so wide.

- The upper half of the archway helps to seal the trap once the trap has fired. Very useful if the seesaw doesn't fit as tightly as it should, if there is too much play on the pivot, or if the animal started to retreat before the seesaw was fully up.

- It helps to support the structure of the trap meaning that the spacing block at the entrance end may not be needed.

- The size of the hole can be adjusted to target or exclude specific species.

Larsen Trap handles & Stilts

This is another simple and brilliant idea that came from one of customers. Moving a Larsen Trap about can be made much easier by the simple addition of handles on the outside. A short length of off cut from the roof lath used for the frame, nailed or screwed to the outside of the top rails makes it much easier to hold.

We also recently had an email from Vaughan in Norfolk with an excellent suggestion for the Larsen Trap design.

"You might find it useful if you fix a triangular piece of wood say 4"x4" x 1.5" on each of the bottom corners to keep it off the ground and stop it rotting over time. It also strengthens it a bit and stops the bird muck from accumulating on the mesh."

An alternative would be to use rails, screwed along the ends or straight across the bottom. These would also strengthen the trap as well as make them easier to stack upside down when not in use. Remember to make the floor using fine mesh, something like 5mm squares, so that the birds can walk on it comfortably and cannot be attacked from underneath.

How to straighten wire

Ever wondered how to get medium and heavy gauge wire straight and ready to work, when it's been supplied on a coil? This suggestion has been supplied by a number of people including Richard from the West Midlands and Mark in Wales and should work on wire up to 3.5mm thick. Cut off lengths of about 4 meters and fix one end - in a vice or similar. Place the other end in the jaws of a cordless drill and gently spin it, twisting the wire. This tensions the wire slightly and pulls it straight, but don't overdo it or you'll start to coil it.

.

More Trap Making – Step by Step

Appendix I - Further Resources

www.fourteenacre.co.uk

This is our own website and shop, provided as a companion to our books and a resource for trap makers worldwide. We supply traps, cage making tools and equipment, trapping accessories, books, DVDs and anything else that we think will be useful to our customers.

As well as further photographs and information on all our plans, any updates will be published here along with feedback, suggestions and experience from other people who have bought and used the book. There is even a Readers Project gallery to share how other trap makers have got on.

Trap Making, Step by Step

By John Bryan

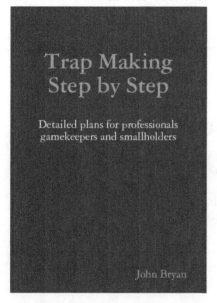

Trap Making, Step by Step has been written for anyone who wants to have a go at making their own traps; from the rural householder to the gamekeeper or farmer.

Based on well proven traditional designs, this book gives simple step by step instructions which enable anyone with basic carpentry skills to make a range of traps. Each chapter also includes a discussion on Options and Variations so that as the readers confidence grows, designs can be modified and developed with completely new ideas.

All of the detailed plans work with light weight wire mesh and wood in sizes that are easy to obtain from any timber yard or builders merchant.

"The book is concise, easy to follow and does exactly what it claims, with a list of tools needed and easy-to-follow plans and diagrams for each trap...This book would be useful to all gamekeepers, but especially to those who are just starting out in the profession and for students, to whom it will be an invaluable source of reference"

National Gamekeepers Organisation - September Magazine

Paperback: 100 pages   Publisher: Fourteenacre Ltd (Jun 2008)   Language: English
ISBN-10: 0955853508   ISBN-13: 978-0955853500   Product Dimensions: 21 x 0.6 x 29.7 cm

Professional Mole Trapping DVD
G.W. Walton

This DVD was filmed and self-produced by Wayne Walton, a full time mole trapper who was catching thousands of moles every year. The filming and production is unquestionably amateur but the real value of this DVD is in the content. What you get is an honest and instructive insight into the craft and techniques of trapping moles - told by a professional in the field, in his own words. The film covers an overview of trap types, trap tuning, mole behaviour (anatomy, tunnels, feeding nesting), trap placement in the field and trap setting. It shows Fenn, Duffus and Talpex type traps in operation.

It is perfect for anyone trying to trap moles for the first time but will also provide the sort of hints and tips that any experienced mole trapper will benefit from.

Running time 101 minutes. Available from Fourteenacre Ltd.

Bodygrip Basics DVD

Specially made to cover "BodyGrip" trapping in the UK, for UK species.

This is essential viewing for pest controllers, trappers, keepers and anyone serious about using these versatile little traps.

The DVD features live footage of Phil Lloyd and Glenn Waters on their trap lines, demonstrating their proven successful sets and methods for 'BodyGrips' and actual catches of Stoat, Squirrel, Mink and Rabbit

Running time 45 minutes. Available from Fourteenacre Ltd

Axholme Wildlife Management Training. (AWM Training)

If you're serious about developing your rural pest control skills, AWM Training provide professional, practical courses in traditional mole trapping, rabbit control and other wildlife management.

www.awmtraining.com

www.vintagetraps.co.uk

Being interested in traps and trap making we at Fourteenacre have a tendency to collect information on old traps and trapping techniques, as well as a few unusual traps themselves. In recent years we have often been contacted by people who are also interested in vintage traps – usually just looking for information, sometimes wanting to buy a particular trap and occasionally with collections to sell. We have built up such a lot of pictures, diagrams and stories that we were struggling to find a way to share them.

Vintagetraps.co.uk is our Virtual Museum and Shop, specially created to properly showcase and sell vintage traps. The whole website is full of pictures and information on every different type of trap that we have come across and we're adding to it all the time.

Sometimes we may only have a picture and only the very basic details, but more often we'll have a good set of images and be able to say quite a lot about it. There are even a good few listed for sale.

Spring Traps Approval Orders

The Spring Traps Approval Orders are available on-line from a variety of websites, but official legislation is available from www.legislation.gov.uk:

There are separate versions for England, Wales, Scotland and Northern Ireland so make sure you're up to date with the correct one for your area.

Other useful websites on UK Trapping:

Natural England: www.naturalengland.org.uk

Game & Wildlife Conservation Trust: www.gwct.org.uk

Dept. for Environment, Food & Rural Affairs: www.defra.gov.uk

Republic of Ireland

National Parks and Wildlife (ROI)   www.npws.ie

Notes

Notes

Notes

Notes

#0111 - 200917 - C0 - 297/210/11 - PB - DID1962969